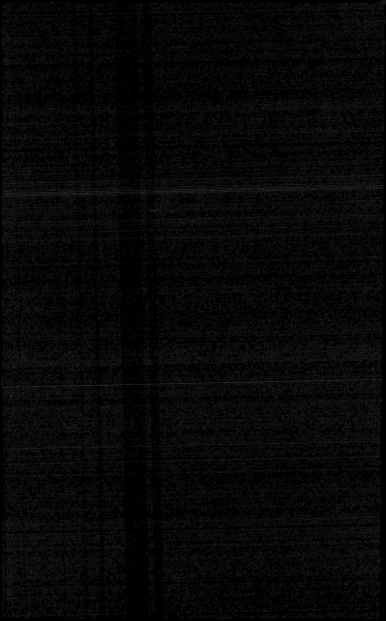

..... an
irreverent
guide to
Texas
Movies

by **Don
Graham**

TCU PRESS • FORT WORTH
A TEXAS SMALL BOOK ★

Library of Congress Cataloging-in-Publication Data

Graham, Don, 1940-
  State fare : an irreverent guide to Texas movies / by Don
Graham.
    p. cm. -- (A Texas small book)
  ISBN 978-0-87565-367-9 (alk. paper)
  1. Texas--In motion pictures. I. Title.

PN1995.9.T47G73 2008
791.43'62764--dc22

                    2007044346

TCU Press
P. O. Box 298300
Fort Worth, TX 76129
817.257.7822
http://www.prs.tcu.edu

To order books: 800.826.8911

Design/Margie Adkins Graphic Design

Dedication

For Betsy, Tommy, & Viv

CONTENTS

★

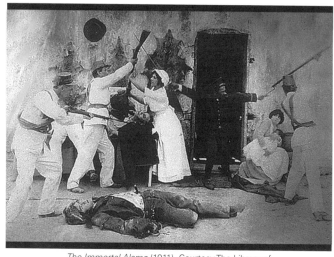

The Immortal Alamo (1911) Courtesy The Library of
the Daughters of the Republic of Texas at the Alamo.

WHEN THE SHOOTING STARTED

The shooting started in Texas on September 24, 1900, when Thomas A. Edison's men made newsreels from ground zero in Galveston, Texas, where the Galveston Hurricane had left a city in ruins. The titles of the flickering footage, such as *Birds-Eye View of Dock Front, Galveston* and *Searching Ruins on Broadway, Galveston, for Dead Bodies*, told the story in moving pictures. Looking back, it seems curious that the very first image of Texas in the movies began with a documentary of disaster, not with the soundless puffs of smoke from silent six-guns.

More predictable fare would come later and would define the image of Texas in movies for a century. From the beginning Texas provided a unique site of major tropes and myths. Texas history was in some ways the equivalent of stories from ancient Britain in Shakespeare's day. The most fecund sources of stories, images, lore, and legend arising from Texas were the lusty men who defended the Alamo, the lusty Texas Rangers who defended the state from Indians and desperadoes, the lusty cowboys who drove the cattle to Kansas, the lusty big ranchers who owned everything, the lusty wildcatters who drilled for oil till they got rich, and even an occasional lusty madam or schoolmarm who stood by their lusty men.

Texas movies in this book mean movies dealing with Texas. They don't have to be made in Texas, and many that have been made in Texas have nothing to do with the state.

The most famous early instance has to be *Wings* (1927), the World War I epic that earned the first Academy Award for "Best Production," later changed to Best Picture. Filmed in San Antonio, miles and miles of trenches were dug to simulate the St. Mihiel battlefield in France, and Texas spruces were spliced to telephone poles to mimic the Lombardy poplars of the French countryside. The big Texas sky where the airplane scenes were shot was left untouched. For the rest of the century Texas stood in for other places. *RoboCop* (1987), for example, was filmed in Dallas, but in the movie Dallas is Detroit, Michigan. Hundred of films made in Texas have nothing to do with Texas. And vice versa.

In fact, the very first Texas movie bore the ultimate Texas title—*Texas Tex* (1908)—and was shot in Copenhagen, Denmark. The production used a troupe of touring Wild West performers that included some authentic American Indians. Billed as an "American story for Americans," it mixed colorful elements of western life, such as capturing and taming wild horses, with rousing melodrama. The plot dealt with a bad cowboy and his sidekick, a Sioux Indian. Never mind that the closest a Sioux ever got to Texas was Sioux City, Iowa. The cowboy steals Tex's horse and abducts his sweetheart. In the woods the bad cowboy tries to kiss the girl, and she resists, whereupon the Sioux kills his partner, hoping to have the girl to himself. But Tex arrives just in time to deck the Indian and reclaim his sweetheart. *Texas Tex* had about as much to do with actual Texas cowboy life as did the scores of singing Westerns with Texas titles made in the 1930s and '40s by Gene Autry, Roy Rogers, and Tex Ritter.

From the beginning of national interest in the West in the late nineteenth century, in actual history and soon to be in film, Texas and Texas cowboys were part of the American dialogue. Through the influence of such figures as Owen Wister, Frederic Remington, and Theodore Roosevelt, the rapidly urbanizing nation was made to revere the cowboy as a picturesque figure, a man of action as well as repose, and perhaps above all, a paragon of American qualities: physical prowess, courage, and a sense of moral rectitude. The cowboy became the American par excellence, and the Texas cowboy, preeminent among cowboys, at least in the number of Westerns made with Texas in the title or with Texas associations. Six percent of all the dime novels of the nineteenth century dealt with Texas, a remarkable statistic in that no other state attained even one percent of such dubious popularity. There have also been over six hundred films with Texas content, well over half of them Westerns.

Scenarists drew their inspiration from a variety of sources: Buffalo Bill's Wild West shows, dime novels, plays, western pulp novels, and sometimes even songs and poems. The results were mostly the same regardless of source: mythology writ large, facts writ small. Nobody wanted to see the real West, most preferred an idealized West, and the Best Western of all those desert motel spaces was Texas, everybody's larger-than-life state of mind.

The first big Western star, Tom Mix, was not from Texas, though Hollywood PR billed him as a former Texas Ranger. Said to hail from El Paso, Mix was in fact from Mix Run, Pennsylvania. Like Davy Crockett, Sam Houston, and many another legendary Texas hero, Mix was a Texan because either (a) he chose to be or (b) studio management thought it was good box office. Mix's success in portraying the Texas cowboy of historical legend and pulp novel popularization can be seen in a number of films. In a film version of Zane Grey's novel *Riders of the Purple Sage* (1925), Mix performed daring deeds in Mormon country, in Utah. A Texas movie? He was a Texas Ranger on a mission to save his niece from a dastardly Mormon bishop who was overly fond of marrying young women. In an earlier film, *The Texan* (1920), Mix portrayed a Texas cowboy who rides over to New Mexico to straighten out a bad situation and save a couple of damsels in distress in the bargain. Said *Motion Picture News*: "Tom Mix is offering propaganda for Texas here and the theme is based upon the specie of male which is raised in the Lone Star state. In other words he appears as a rip-snorting, 'up and at 'em,' hard-riding, six-shooting cowboy who will show the neighbors over in New Mexico just what constitutes a regular he-man!"

The first significant movie made in Texas was not a cowboy picture; it was a film about the Alamo that went back to the core mythology of Texas' founding for its story line and inspiration. Gaston Méliès, a Frenchman, produced it. Méliès' brother Charles had made many movies in France in the earliest days of the new medium, including the well-known *A Trip to the Moon*. Gaston Méliès moved to New York where he filmed "actualities," real events such as Theodore Roosevelt's 1905 inauguration. Eventually he started his own production company, the Star

Film Ranch, in San Antonio, where from 1910–1911 he made over seventy films, only three of which have survived. Some were Westerns or Texas-themed, such as *The Cowboy and the Rancher Girl* (1910), *A Texas Joke* (1910), and *Tony, the Greaser* (1911). But it was *The Immortal Alamo* in 1911 that has always drawn the most attention and is the one we know the most about. It was certainly the most fitting film to be shot in the Alamo City. Professional actors included Francis Ford, John Ford's brother, along with amateurs such as students from the Peacock Military Academy who played Santa Anna's soldiers. Though the film has not survived, there are a number of extant stills that suggest its content. One depicts a coonskin-cap-wearing figure with a long rifle: obviously Davy Crockett. Another depicts an action scene showing Susannah Dickinson and her infant-in-arms being spared from slaughter.

Despite Gaston Méliès' valiant efforts to turn San Antonio into a mecca of moviemaking, it was another town in the West, Hollywood, that soon dominated the nascent film industry. In fact, that was where Méliès himself moved, in late 1911. By 1913 movie product began to pour out of the little L.A. suburb.

Even so, Texas remained a well-defined movie state. In one ten-year period, from 1921 through 1930, more films were made with Texas titles, content, or settings than was true of any other state. Texas led with eighty-eight movies; California was next with seventy-one. Arizona was third with fifty-five. Other Western states trailed far behind: Kansas, sixteen; Wyoming, fourteen; Oregon, ten, New Mexico, six.

By the time the silents were over, every major Texas subject and theme had been turned into a film: Besides the Alamo, there were movies about early Texas history, trail drives, ranches, oil, women, and comic Texans. What was left? Sex, Football, and NASA.

It is not possible to see all the known films about Texas. Many silents are lost, having suffered "nitrate death." Of the twenty-one films about Texas released in 1925–26, for example, nineteen are lost. Fortunately, four of the big Texas films of the silent era have survived. ★

THE STRONG, SILENT TYPE
Martyrs of the Alamo; or the Birth of Texas, 1915

W. Christy Cabanne, one of the most prolific directors of films in Hollywood history—and among the dullest, according to one film historian—helmed 166 films from the early silent era onward. In 1915, Cabanne had a very big year indeed. He was an (uncredited) assistant director on D. W. Griffith's sensational *The Birth of a Nation; Or The Clansman* (1915). This famous, epoch-making film, which President Woodrow Wilson proclaimed as "history written in lightning," must have had a marked influence on Cabanne. Griffith was the "supervisor" (producer) of Cabanne's *Alamo* film, which in effect translated Griffith's southern racial/sexual into racial/sexual politics set in Texas. In a running time of fifty minutes, Cabanne painted the struggle for Texas independence in lurid stereotypes.

Martyrs turns the entire battle for Texas into a racial conflict between brown and white. Although the prologue to the film explains the familiar historical reasons for the battle—Santa Anna's tyranny, the Texans' love of freedom—the film itself focuses on the clash between races. Mexican soldiers in San Antonio routinely insult any Anglo woman who comes into view. As one title puts it, "Under the dictator's rule the honor and life of American womanhood was held in contempt." The Texans are all Anglos; there are no Tejanos on the Anglo side in this version. The Texans grow angrier with each insult, more resolved than ever to resist Santa Anna's tyranny. At the same time the level of Mexican arrogance increases. Soldiers hold cock fights in the streets; they perform hat dances at every opportunity. Santa Anna himself is portrayed as the prototype of degeneracy: "An inveterate drug fiend, the Dictator of Mexico [is] also famous for his shameless orgies."

In this film, of course, the Anglo Texans are noble beyond the saying of it—from moccasined feet to coonskin caps. (There are so many coonskins in some scenes that it's hard to tell which one is Davy Crockett.) The Anglo Texans are handsome, brave, loyal, patriotic, and polite to womenfolk. In fact, they're just like all the Alamo heroes until we get to the last one, 2004's *The Alamo*, when the Big Three are given feats of clay.

Once the battle begins, the film hews to a steady action course and contains fairly impressive scenes of carnage both inside and outside the walls of the old mission. Bowie's death, for example, follows the legendary story effectively.

Martyrs of the Alamo (1915) Triangle Film Corp.; Courtesy Wisconsin Center for Film and Theater Research.

According to long-standing tradition, the bedridden Bowie was impaled in the chest by Mexican bayonets but not before he had dispatched a large number of enemy soldiers. So it is in the film.

But even in the battle scenes the racial ideology prevails. Mexican officers have to shoot their own craven soldiers to keep them from fleeing to the nearby San Antonio river. The most inflammatory instance of racial portrayal, reminiscent of *The Birth of a Nation*, occurs as the attackers swarm into the courtyard. A Mexican soldier seizes a wide-eyed little blonde female American child and dashes her to death against a wall. The Texans fight on.

Once the Alamo has fallen, Santa Anna spares a few survivors. One is Mrs. Dickinson (fact) and another is a pretty, blonde heroine (fiction). He casts his lecherous eyes upon the blonde, but she cuffs him on the ear for making advances.

The film ends with the Texans' victory at San Jacinto. Here again, Santa Anna's rapacious sexual appetite is a dominant part of his character. While Sam Houston's forces are gathering for attack, Santa Anna is engaged in another orgy and oblivious to the approaching danger. Here, the film reprises the Emily Morgan "Yellow Rose of Texas" legend, another bit of folkloristic history based itself on racial lines. Emily Morgan was a mulatto with whom Santa Anna is supposed to have had a dalliance that fatal April afternoon. It takes Houston's army only a short time (true: eighteen minutes) to rout the Mexican troops, and Texas independence—and racial purity—is assured. The movie ends with a succession of flags over Texas: the 1824 Mexican flag, the Lone Star of the Republic, the Confederate, and the U.S.

In the early 1920s a Texas movie distributor re-released *Martyrs of the Alamo* under the title *The Birth of Texas,* hoping to play off the famous Griffith film and hoping as well to rekindle some traditional Texas patriotism. In some parts of the state, however, the strategy backfired. In Baytown, for example, Mexican-American citizens, outraged at the film's blatant racism, walked out of the theater in protest. From the beginning, the Alamo has been one of the most tendentious and explosive subjects that a filmmaker could touch. Nothing has changed in the past eighty-nine years. ★

North of 36, 1924

North of 36, the first major cattle drive film, was shot partly on location on a ranch thirty miles from Houston and in many frames carries a very authentic flavor. In one shot, for instance, the cattle are being driven through a shallow, dry arroyo and in the background are trees with Spanish moss, something you don't see in those "Texas" films shot in Arizona. The other authentic element in *North of 36* is the cattle themselves, five thousand longhorns were used in the making of the film. J. Frank Dobie, no admirer of shoot-em-ups, liked the realistic way in which cattle were handled in this film, as he wrote in *Cow People:* "Often in recollection I see the lead steer, Old Alamo, a mighty longhorn, dun in color, standing at the edge of a lake where the other steers were standing, watering. They looked serene, as cattle at water usually are." He also liked the fact that the cattle were walked at a leisurely pace, as in the old days of the real cattle drives. Cattle were the most romantic critters in Texas history, and cowboys, their tender tenders, were the most romantic of Texas heroes. It was a perfect fit.

After the Civil War, ranchers in Texas had plenty of land and cattle, but little money. What they needed were markets for their cattle, and the burgeoning beef industry in Chicago needed meat on the hoof, and then came a solution: the establishment of railheads in Missouri, Kansas and Nebraska. Although the cattle drive period lasted only a short time, from 1867 to 1885, the romance of the trail played a huge role in the creation of an appealing myth of economic salvation and triumphant nationalism. The grand intentions of *North of 36* are what make it the archetype of all subsequent cattle-drive epics. Among the prologue titles was a quotation from historian Phillip Aston Rollins that might have explained every cattle drive movie: "The Texas Trail was no mere cowpath. It was the course of Empire."

With such premises in mind, *North of 36* depended upon a shaky plot structure to dramatize these values. Taisie Lockhart, the willowy young heroine, played by Lois Wilson, has lost her father, a rancher, to a Yankee carpetbagger's cowardly bullet, leaving her with a ranch, thousands of cattle, but no cash. She's so broke she can't pay her ranch hands but the cowpokes admire her so much they're willing to work for nothing, to risk everything on a trail drive north to railheads

North of 36, 1924 Paramount; Courtesy Museum of Modern Art, Film Stills Archive.

11

in Kansas, north of the 36th parallel. So Taisie puts on her best trail-driving outfit, saddles up her pinto pony, and with an old geezer sidekick and a band of loyal cowboys, sets out to find new markets for Texas beef.

The unmarked prairie trail is long and filled with danger, and it's clear from early in the film that she is going to need the gunfighterly skills of a tall, dark, handsome hero named Dan McMasters (Jack Holt), to help her and the herd out of various jams. But she misunderstands the hero's intentions, and so for most of the drive he has to provide help sort of in absentia, operating on the fringes, doing what he can to erase difficulties and overcome obstacles. The biggest impediment is the state treasurer of Texas, a Yankee carpetbagger appointed by a punitive Yankee government, and the very man, it turns out, who murdered Taisie's father. He wants her ranch and will stop at nothing to accomplish his nefarious ends. Pardon the melodramatic language, but with fat, oily villains who wear black suits and smoke big cigars, you find yourself falling back on adjectives like nefarious to describe them. This villain is so despicable that in a sub-plot, he comes upon two Comanche women bathing nude in a stream (the silents took a sort of *National Geographic* view of unclothed native women), and he rapes one of them. The title for this sequence is "Virgin Wilderness." Later at film's end, the villain is turned over to the Comanches, who make fajitas out of him.

After overcoming the standard number of problems, including a grass fire, a river crossing, stampedes, Comanche attacks, and raids by outlaws, Taisie and her cowboys, with the help of the two-gun hero, reach Abilene, Kansas, and deliver the first herd to that emerging boom town, driving the cattle down the middle of the street. The epic drive accomplishes exactly what McMasters foresaw: "The North and the South are going to build a new world above the old slavery line! It will be the West—the heart of America."

North of 36 wasn't the only cattle drive movie of 1924, however. That same year there appeared a film called *Sundown*, directed by Harry O. Hoyt and Lawrence Trimble. Running ninety minutes, it told the story of cattlemen fighting off the attempts of nestors to overrun their lands and steal their herds. Though the film has not survived, it seems to have been a notable effort to capture the majesty of the trail drive enterprise. One still photograph is truly remarkable: a herd of cattle is stretched across the plains in a leisurely line, issuing out of nowhere and headed to some remote destination. There are no cowboys in the scene, no barbed wire, no 7–11's, no mobile homes, nothing but land, sky, and cattle. A reviewer for the *New York Times* found the story "unusually boring" but admired the "impressive scenes of thousands and thousands of cattle." The reviewer added, "As we heard someone say, this picture is all very well if you like cows." Moo-vie cows would be a staple of Texas Westerns for the rest of the century.

North of 36 was filmed twice more, as *The Conquering Herd* in 1931 and as *The Texans* in 1938. Shot on location near Cotulla, *The Texans* attracted the attention of J. Frank Dobie, who happened to be in L.A. when the film was released. When he saw a poster announcing a film about his home state and his favorite subject, cowboys and cattle, he bought a ticket to see it. Instead of the cattle walking as they had in the old silent film, these ran madly all the way to Kansas. Dobie was disgusted.

It wouldn't be until 1948's *Red River,* that Hollywood finally got a handle on the cattle drive movie and got it right. ★

A Texas Steer, 1927

In 1898 a brief sequence titled *A Texas Steer* was shot at Swift & Co.'s stockyard in Chicago, depicting some stockyard "matadors" having fun with a wild steer. The title derived from Charles Hoyt's popular play of 1890, *A Texas Steer.* In 1915 a theatrical film based on the play starred Tyrone Power Sr. and Mrs. Tyrone Power, the parents of the American film star, Tyrone Power. The play was filmed a second time, in 1927, starring Will Rogers. (Unfortunately, both films are lost). The Rogers version is the most important representation of the comic Texan in the Silent Era. The Texas steer, Maverick Brander, is a cattleman turned congressman. Brander hails from Red Dog, Texas, "where men are men and the plumbing is improving," and he wonders after his election, "I'm an honest man—what will I do in Congress?"

Once installed in Washington, he continues to wear his ranchman's garb and keeps being mistaken for a member of a Wild West troupe. Unlike his fellow Congressmen, he advocates "more wisdom and less wind." Brander's slightly vulgar wife and his high-spirited daughter, Bossy, who calls herself "a gawky Texas girl in a frightful dress," round out this Texas family that strikes official Washington as not "tame." After a couple of years, though, the Branders win acceptance, thanks in large part to their wealth.

While Brander learns to dress less flamboyantly, the rougher side of his Texas background remains in high relief through the presence of three rowdy Texas cronies: Yell, Bragg, and Blow. Yell is a "great-boned" Texan, and Bragg and Blow "look as much like Yell as possible." (Chill Wills became the prototype of this type of comic Texan in the talkies.) Their names indicate their characters. They are loud,

A Texas Steer, 1927. First National Pictures; Courtesy Museum of Modern Art, Film Stills Archive.

they like to brag—about Texas, of course—and they like to "blow"—talk. They never adjust their Wild West hyperbole to the usages of polite society. During a fancy dinner party late in the play, Yell, Bragg, and Blow break out their pistols and start a riot.

The impact of Brander's tenure in Congress can be seen in a paean to the greatness of Texas. Brassy Gall, a conniving Washington lobbyist, tries to enlist Brander's support in a pork-barrel project: "The time was when we regarded Texas as the refuge of the criminal and the home of the coyote—but since Mr. Brander arrived our eyes have been opened. We have learned to appreciate the greatness and future glory of Texas! He has taught us that Texas is the coming Empire State! Gentlemen, thanks to the efforts of Mr. Brander, Texas is becoming the center of commerce and home of Science, Literature, and the Arts!"

Yell, who by this time is drunk, interrupts with a cry, "Three cheers for literature!" Then Gall continues, "And mark my words, gentlemen, in five years—and maybe less— New York will go to Texas for its fashions." That prediction wouldn't come true for a few decades.

Will Rogers breathed an air of naturalness into Maverick Brander and won plaudits from the *New York Times*. Rogers also wrote most of the titles and did a fine job of capturing the vernacular humor of the original. Play and movies, *A Texas Steer* remains one of the key early vehicles for transmitting the image of Texas to a large audience. As late as 1939, the play was still in print for the express purpose of fostering contemporary productions. ★

The Wind, 1928

A classic of the silent era, *The Wind* was the first Texas film to build an entire story around a female character. The novel on which the film was based, Dorothy Scarborough's *The Wind,* created something of a local sensation upon its appearance in 1925. Set near the West Texas town of Sweetwater, it was denounced by the Sweetwater Chamber of Commerce as well as many West Texas newspapers for its depiction of Texas weather. "The wind was the cause of it all," the novel begins. Curiously, Edna Ferber, who would later, in *Giant,* present her own controversial portrait of Texas, was the one who encouraged young Dorothy Scarborough to write a story of the conditions under which frontier women lived on the Texas plains. Republished in 1979, *The Wind* won a new generation of readers—chiefly for its feminist thrust.

The Mojave Desert, where the film was shot, was supposed to be West Texas, and the star, Lillian Gish, remembered it as "the very worst experience I ever went through." Blowing sand and intense sun replicated the plains setting of nineteenth century Texas when, Scarborough wrote, "there was nothing to break the sweep of the wind across the treeless prairies." Into this harsh environment comes Letty, a young woman from Virginia who joins her married cousin's family and tries to build a life for herself. Besides the constant wind, there is the gritty sand that gets into everything: canisters, clothes, bedsheets. Then there are the people. Her cousin Cora (Dorothy Cumming) is jealous of Letty's gentililty and softness, and the men are at best half-civilized. This is the theme of the film: the attempt to maintain Eastern/Southern civilization in the midst of a crude, brutish frontier where nature's violence, unremitting toil, and primitive conditions are the order of existence.

Cora is already defeated. She has three kids and is bitter and envious. She tells Letty exactly what her options are: she must marry and marry quickly if she wants to survive, for Cora will not permit her to remain in her home. So Letty does what she has to; she chooses between two suitors, a young cowpoke named Lige and an old-timer named Sourdough. She picks Lige (Lars Hanson), and their honeymoon is one of the film's finest scenes. He brings her through the howling wind to a bare-as-bones cabin that has plain wooden walls decorated only with animal skins, a table littered with kitchen remains, and a bed full of sand. Their marriage remains unconsummated as Letty, who married solely to survive, shrinks from any physical contact with her new husband. Lige vows to save enough money to send her back East where she belongs. When she looks at some stereoptican slides, Letty remembers what life used to be like. One shows her standing beside a bush in her native Virginia. But she's not in Virginia now, and the days pass, as the title announces, in a blur of "Wind Sand Wind Sand Yesterday Tomorrow Forever."

With Lige absent much of the time, Letty grows increasingly nervous from the solitude and the wind. Then temptation comes in the form of Wirt Roddy (Montagu Love), a traveling salesman, a married man, whom she met on the train to Sweetwater and who has offered to "keep" her. She twice resists Roddy's entreaties, and in the last instance accidentally shoots him to death when he tries to assault her. Lige returns and accepts her explanation of what happened, and in the closing scene, standing at the door of their cabin in a pile of sand, she pledges her love to Lige in rather astounding terms, considering her earlier distaste: "I'm not afraid of anything now, because I'm your wife, to work with you, to love you."

This ending, the kind that early on came to be called the Hollywood ending, is 100 percent different from what happens in the novel. In it, Letty, desperate, frightened, sleeps with Wirt Roddy, then kills him and wanders into the desert to let the sands cover her as well. Thus one death and another one to come mark the closing of the novel, bringing the tragedy to its inexorable end.
The director of the film,
Victor Sjöström,

The Wind, 1928
MGM; Courtesy Museum of Modern Art, Film Stills Archive.

who belongs in the company of Carl Dreyer and Ingmar Bergman as the three premier Scandinavian filmmakers, faithfully shot the novel's ending, but MGM preferred a happier finale, and the scene was re-shot for the sake of audience satisfaction. Even so, *The Wind* holds up today as a powerful silent picture of arduous frontier conditions for women living on the Texas plains. And the point remains, regardless of the false ending, that Letty is already doomed to Cora's fate. In fact, Wirt Roddy was correct when he said she had already become a "farm wife." The film's status is secure. As Robert Sklar puts it in *Movie-Made America*, *The Wind* is an "extraordinary work of cinema naturalism." ★

A Handful of Texas Steers

When sound came along, at the end of the twenties, the studios formalized a two-tier system that had already begun to develop in the silent era: (1) major productions with big stars, big budgets, and big ambitions; and (2) smaller productions, B movies, quickies shot in a couple of weeks or so, with bottom basement scripts and almost no ambitions at all. The B's were the bread-and-butter of the big studios and the mainstay of the smaller studios like Republic and Monogram. The B's were fun, wacky, and forgettable, except for a few accidental gems. Following are five steers from a herd of thousands of Saturday matinee shoot-em-ups that blazed across the theaters of the nation in the 1930s , '40s, and '50s. ★

The Big Show, 1936

The Big Show, starring Gene Autry, was unusual in several respects. First, it was partially filmed on location in Texas, at the State Fair Grounds in Dallas, during the Centennial Exhibition. As a result, several shots show the art deco buildings as they looked in 1936, the SMU marching band, the famed stripper Sally Rand, and various crowd scenes of people attending the fair. *The Big Show* thus has an accidental documentary value today. Of particular interest are scenes from the Cavalcade of Texas, a popular spectacle featuring 300 actors in an historical pageant designed to reveal the "glamour of Lone Star State history," from "conquistador to cowboy, from the quest for gold to the discovery of oil."

The movie wove together plot strands into the texture of the local setting in clever ways. In one exciting episode of the Cavalcade, Gene is racing after outlaws on his famous horse Champion, when the horse falls, his leg apparently broken. Then Gene stands over the body of his beloved steed and sings a song of farewell, "Old Faithful, we rode the range together." Then he points his pistol at Champion and just when it looks as though he's going to pull the trigger, Champion playfully wags his head and rises to stand up, while the audience breaks into relieved applause. This is really horse opera.

The other unusual aspect of the film is its complex plot structure and self-reflexive commentary on musical Westerns and B movies in general. Gene Autry plays two parts: an unknown stunt man and double for a snooty B movie star named Tom Ford, and Tom Ford. They both work for Mammoth Studio—a jibe at the big studios—and in the opening scene, on a Western movie set in California, we see how nice Gene is and how obnoxious Ford is. When Ford goes to kiss his leading lady, she accuses him of having onions on his breath. Even his horse dislikes him and takes a bite out of his rear end.

When Tom Ford refuses to go to Dallas to shoot his next film, the studio hires his double to go in his place. Gene stands out as a stand in, singing songs that get played on the radio and foiling the machinations of some gangster types who are trying to collect a gambling debt from Ford. Gene Autry emerges as a star on all counts (he can sing and Ford cannot), and a Mammoth studio exec announces, "From now on we're making nothing but musical Westerns." At film's end they are back in California shooting a Western with Ford doubling for Autry, who croons to Ford's former co-star, "I'm Just Mad About You." This kind of playfulness enlivens the film throughout.

The Big Show charms us with its playful mix of on-location color, genre hijinks, and sly industry humor. It remains a triumph of low-budget studio inventiveness and a rebuke to anybody who wants to dismiss the lowly B western out of hand. The film also contains an uncredited appearance by Leonard Sly (known to history as Roy Rogers) who appears with the group Sons of the Pioneers. Rogers and his bride Dale Evans honeymooned in Dallas during the filming. ★

Heroes of the Alamo, 1937

B movies rarely undertook epic-sized subjects, but one notable exception is this seventy-five-minute opus released one year after the Texas Centennial. Curiously, it is one of the most interesting of that subgenre, the Alamo film, that has produced a string of boring, bloated, rhetorically flatulent films down through the decades from the silents into the twenty-first century.

Heroes of the Alamo, directed by Harry L. Fraser, admittedly has laughable production values. All the Alamo defenders dress like conventional cowboys, and the town of San Antonio looks like a standard issue back lot Western town, which of course is where it was filmed. And there are some odd riffs on the traditional iconography of the Alamo story. Colonel Travis, for example, draws the famous line in the sand with his rifle butt instead of a sword, and Davy Crockett, a somewhat crazed old coot in this version, dies without any big build-up or heroics. But what makes this film one of the more interesting slices of the pie Alamo is its highly original focus on a simple, uncelebrated man. Instead of memorializing the predictable triad of heroes, Travis, Bowie, Crockett (or one of them), it democratizes the Alamo by making a minor figure, Almaron Dickinson (Bruce Warren), the center of the drama. Dickinson, a farmer, decided it was his duty to stand and die at the Alamo, and the cost is especially personal, as he must say goodbye to his wife, Susannah Dickinson (Ruth Finley), and their infant, both of whom were spared from death

23

by Santa Anna. Thus in this film we see something of the sacrifice made by an ordinary man, not a legendary hero, to make Texas safe for Texans.

One of the best moments in the film is an historical anachronism. The night before the final assault by the Mexican army, the Texans, wearing their cowboy hats, sing "The Yellow Rose of Texas." The problem is, this song wasn't written until 1857. Even more interesting, they sing the original minstrel version of the song, which contains explicit racialist language that goes back to the origins of the lyric in the legend of mulatto Emily Morgan's presumed dalliance with Santa Anna on the afternoon of April 21, 1836, just before the Battle of San Jacinto was fought. Typical lines include: "She's the sweetest little darkie that Texas ever knew" and "She's the sweetest rose of color that Texas ever knew." Using this version says a lot about the atmosphere of racial dialogue in Hollywood in the 1930s. ★

Three Texas Steers, 1939

If one Texas steer was good, three must be better: so must have gone the reasoning behind the title of this 1939 oater. But it does seem odd that a steer, a castrated bovine, represents the image of the Texas macho male. It's probably because nobody knew what a steer was.

The main steer in this film is none other than John Wayne, who six months earlier had finally got a break-out role, in John Ford's *Stagecoach* (1939), and escaped, or so he thought, the ignominy of starring in B's. But Republic Studio, the famed Poverty Row factory, used Wayne's new fame in *Stagecoach* to sell tickets to *Three Texas Steers.* Needless to say, Wayne resented the ploy, and he wanted to forget films like *Three Texas Steers,* which he had been bogged down in all through the 1930s.

In this film there are three leads: the Three Mesquiteers, a parody of the famous French trio. Wayne as Stony Brooke rides a white horse and has two sidekicks: Tucson Smith (Ray Lonigan) and Lullaby Joslin (Max Terhune). Terhune is supposed to supply the comedy, and in a couple of scenes brings his wooden dummy Elmer in for a few yuks. There is also some comedy involving Wayne, of the usual corny kind found in the B's: A girl named Lillian asks him, "What's your job?" to which he replies, "I'm a

Three Texas Steers (1939) Republic; Courtesy Wisconsin Center for Film and Theater Research.

25

cowhand, ma'am. I chase cows," to which she fires back: "If I could only learn to moo."

Most of the action takes place in Mesquite County, Texas. The plot develops from the misfortunes of a circus owned by Nancy Evans (Carole Landis), a nice, leggy brunette. Her manager has eyes on a ranch she owns and tries to force her to sell it by creating accidents that bankrupt her circus. But Nancy and her entourage go to Mesquite County to lick their wounds. She brings quite a group to the ranch: a sassy blonde, Hercules the Midget, a young male circus trapeze artist, an ape, and a horse that waltzes to the tune of "The Blue Danube." By mistake they settle in at the wrong ranch, one owned by the Three Mesquiteers. Misunderstandings multiply until finally the Mesquiteers steal Rajah the Wonder Horse in order to win a harness-trotting race, expose the villains, and launch Nancy and company back into the circus business.

Besides the ape, this movie also has a small armored vehicle with tracks like a tank that is used to pull a covered wagon containing Rajah the Wonder Horse. What armored vehicles, apes, and harness races have to do with Texas is not evident. The big harness racing scene at the Mesquite County Fair is a perfect example of the incongruous mix of elements in this film—and in many B Westerns. Indeed, incongruity is a norm of the B Western. Here, hundreds of well-dressed Eastern types watch the race, while in the rest of the town scenes the sheriff and others look like hayseed cowboys. This ridiculous story line took fifty-six minutes to unfold, a typical length for B westerns. ★

Texas To Bataan, 1942

The seventeenth of twenty-four films in the "Range Buster" series put out by Monogram, a leading B studio, *Texas to Bataan* starred the now almost totally forgotten John "Dusty" King, who plays Dusty King in this strange World War II-themed B Western. John King, a former band leader and singer, appeared in an assortment of B Westerns and other cheapie genre films such as those in the Mr. Moto and Charlie Chan series.

The comic Max Terhune also turns up in *Texas to Bataan* billed as Alibi Terhune. His dummy Elmer is listed in the credits as "Alibi's dummy." Separately or together, they're still not funny. The third member of the Range Busters was David Sharpe, who plays Davey Sharpe. A National Tumbling Champion when he was just fifteen, Sharpe appeared in 199 films as a stunt man and as an actor, often in bit parts, in 154 films.

An early scene announces the political propaganda theme in unmistakable terms. Alibi discovers—out of the blue, apparently—two silhouette targets of Adolph Hitler and Benito Mussolini. He begins blazing away, and his Range Buster buddies, Dusty and Davey, join him, exclaiming, "Massacre them" and "Blow 'em down."

After this start, the plot gets complicated fast. Local ranchers, who are raising beef and horses for the army, are reporting heavy losses from theft. Although America isn't in the war yet, an air of crisis intensifies the usual B problem of stolen livestock. After all, one rancher avers, "There's a war going on in Europe." The Range Busters swing into action and capture three cattle thieves, but Cookie, a suspicious-looking Asian who works for the head rancher, turns them loose, then vanishes. Letters found in his room prove that he's a Japanese spy. Fortunately for the fate of the western democracies, the Range Busters recapture the escaped outlaws.

In the Bataan half of the movie, the Range Busters go to the Philippines to oversee the delivery of horses to the U.S. Army stationed there. They don't leave their musical talents at home. In a Filipino bamboo café, the Range Busters serenade the locals with a rendition of "Home on the Range." The locals love it. Then guess who walks into the café—Cookie, the Japanese spy. Although one of the Range Busters says this is a job for the FBI, another sees it as RB business and follows Cookie up to his room where, it turns out, he's in constant radio contact with Tokyo. A fight breaks out and spreads to the café/saloon, where a general melee ensues. The Asians are easily distinguishable from the Range Busters because they don't wear cowboy hats and they throw a lot of knives. Obviously they are just like typical ethnic villains in Westerns set in Texas, and it's no big deal for the Range Busters to bust them. But the MP's mistakenly arrest the heroes, who quickly report that they overheard plans "to dynamite our vital harbors." Appreciative of their detective work, the army lets them go and urges them to find the traitor in Texas—Cookie's American contact—and "corral him Texas style."

Back in Texas they do this. With spies safely in jail, the boys enjoy a quite Sunday at the ranch, reading the funnies and preparing to go to church with the rancher's pretty daughter. Then a radio news bulletin announces that Japanese planes have bombed Pearl Harbor! Resolved to "go all the way to Tokyo," the boys will first go to church. The movie ends with a promise: "We'll be seeing you in our next picture." ★

Terror In A Texas Town, 1958

Regarded by several critics as the greatest B Western ever made, this film is a real treat for lovers of the Western genre. It subverts many conventions while following the main lines of the formula of outlaws being made to pay for injustices committed against the innocent. Directed by Joseph H. Lewis, the celebrated B auteur of such works as *Gun Crazy* (1949), the film was scripted by an even more famous writer, Dalton Trumbo, the best-known of the blacklisted Hollywood Ten and cited in the credits as Millard Kaufman to avoid detection.

Terror in a Texas Town (1958)
Courtesy Frank Selzer
Productions Inc.

The plot is the familiar one of a land grab by an oily banker (Sebastian Cabot) who has hired a gunfighter, Johnny Crale (Ned Young), to do the dirty work. Young dresses entirely in black, as required by the rules of the genre, but he has an artificial hand, is impotent, and enjoys lobster dinners right there in the middle of a landlocked nowhere. His adversary on the other side of the line is George Hansen, played by Sterling Hayden. Hayden has returned to this conventional Western town to deal with the consequences of his father's death. His father, of course, was killed by the gunfighter on the banker's orders because oil has been discovered on the family ranch. (The discovery of oil in Texas is thus moved to an earlier date, in the 1880s or so.) Another surprise is that the neighboring ranch is owned by a Mexican family.

But the biggest surprise of all is the showdown on Main Street, site of hundreds of showdowns in Western movies. As the menacing gunfighter moves toward Hayden, we discover that Hayden's weapon of choice is a harpoon! Why? Because he is a whaling captain and has been off on the high seas chasing giant whales. Hayden dispatches the gunfighter with ease in the most unlikely fast draw/fast harpoon duel in the history of the movies.

Anybody who read the posters for this film in 1958 would have had some inkling of what was coming. "Iron-Hooked Fury" read one pitch, and "Harpoon Against Six-Gun for the Black Gold that flowed under the blood-drenched sand" read another. Everything about this film is weird: the music, which sounds like pre-Spaghetti Western music; the empty streets of a town where almost no one seems to live (because of a very scant budget, Lewis didn't hire extras); and those strange mannerisms and weapons. This was Lewis' last feature film. ★

GRADE A TEXAS BEEF

Truly iconic Texas films, the ones that most powerfully defined the state as a mythic site, were all Westerns or had strong Western associations. This is not surprising since Texas and the Western had been wedded from the beginning of cinema. ". . .if you go to Texas—go on a horse with a gun." To Darryl Zanuck, the Texas landscape dictated an action picture, not a psychological study of grief. It dictated a Western.

The big Texas movies all followed the Western formula, and the top four in mythic grandeur appeared during the period of Texas' most pronounced national visibility, the years following World War II. Those were the years that saw the apotheosis of King Ranch, of Big Oil, of Texan War Hero Audie Murphy, of Lyndon Johnson in the U.S. Senate, of billionaires like H. L. Hunt, of Neiman Marcus. Three of the four films appeared between 1948 and 1963, the arc of national ascension that marked the rise of Texas as a Super-State, to adapt the title of John Bainbridge's 1961 book on Texans, *The Super-Americans.* The films are *Red River* (1948), *Giant* (1956), *Hud* (1963), and *The Last Picture Show* (1971). No Texas films before are

31

as rich as these and few afterwards come close.

Taken together as a continuous narrative of myth-making, this four of a kind defines the founding, the growth of empire, the ironic decline, and the death of the central trope of Texas film mythology: the cattle kingdom in all its glory. ★

Red River, 1948

Red River, which begins the cycle, is the story of the founding of a world. It is an Anglo version of that founding. Tom Dunson (John Wayne) crosses the Red River, abandoning his sweetheart, leaving her for land. Land is more important than any human tie, more important even than the love of a good woman. (It's true, of course, that she is supposed to join him later, but is killed in an Indian attack before doing so.) South of Red River, 200 miles from the Rio Bravo, Dunson performs the primal act. He takes the land away from its owners, a Mexican grandee. The Mexican owns too much land for any man to possess, says Old Groot, Wayne's sidekick (Walter Brennan), and besides, as Groot explains, the Mexican had taken it away from somebody else anyway. Then follows the story of expansionism and of a changing world, the new phase of distant markets and finance capitalism, a world that Dunson does not understand. It remains for his adopted son (Montgomery Clift) to lead the trail herd to the new site of capitalism, the railheads at Abilene, Kansas, where Joseph McCoy had prepared the ground for the mass marketing of cattle ultimately bound for the Chicago slaughter houses and transformation into expensive steaks at Delmonico's in New York City or into canned tins of Vienna Sausage for cowboys back in Texas. Through some tricky plot manipulations, Wayne and Clift are reconciled, and the empire's line of succession is secure. The ranch will be passed on to the next generation, which has proved itself worthy. No later movies are as confident of the line of succession as is *Red River*. ★

Red River (1948) Courtesy Charles K. Feldman Group

Giant, 1956

In *Giant* the ranch founded by Wayne—symbolically speaking—is now a huge feudal patriarchy with its lord—Bick Benedict (Rock Hudson)—its lady, Leslie Benedict (Elizabeth Taylor)—and a work force of cowboys and peasants, the latter all having one thing in common: they are of Mexican ancestry. *Giant* is a kind of dreamscape of the ranching tradition as it would like to see itself, and it embodies every element of the archetypal Texas movie: it contains cowboys, wildcatters, cattle, empire, wealth, crassness of manners, garish taste, drawling speech, and barbeque. But the world of *Giant* is undergoing tremendous pressures to change, and the conditions for change are imminent. Unlike *Red River,* in which the woman is a purely symbolic figure, in *Giant* the woman is vitally present; and she represents both a criticism of Texas patriarchy and a grudging accommodation with Texas' provincial power. Leslie Benedict challenges the old ways but eventually, through her long-running marriage, makes a number of concessions to the weight of tradition. But the biggest challenge to the wholeness of the ranching way of life is irresponsible materialism as represented by the

Giant (1956) Courtesy Warner Bros.

ruthless young wildcatter, Jett Rink, played beguilingly by James Dean in his last film. Dean's heavy Method acting seems to belong to another movie, but he manages to steal most of the scenes he's in.

Oil, and the glittering, easy wealth that it engenders, is the force that is reshaping modern post-War Texas. The ranchers resist the incursions of oil, and then, once it's found on their land, appreciate its capacity for generating great sums of money. At the same time, *Giant's* feudalism—specifically in the form of oppressive racial injustice—remains painfully intact, despite Leslie's attempts to improve the lot of Mexican-American laborers, and her son's marriage to a Mexican woman and his decision to become a doctor and practice medicine among the disadvantaged living in the very shadow of Reata. Bick Benedict's rousing fight in the diner as "The Yellow Rose of Texas" pounds out of the jukebox is an important moment in the film, and in Texas film history, when, though defeated physically, the aging rancher achieves a moral triumph in publicly acknowledging the fact that his grandson, of mixed descent, is a Benedict. (In the scene in the novel, Bick is not present, and no fight occurs.) *Giant* was a huge favorite in Texas for at least two generations, and did more than any other single film to define what Texas looked like for the rest of the world, especially those who had never been to the state. Kirby Warnock's documentary film, *Return to Giant* (2003), lovingly recreates the making of the movie in Marfa and surrounds and offers commentary on the film's continuing importance as a cultural document. ★

Hud, 1963

Just seven years later, in the year of the assassination of JFK, a much darker Western, *Hud,* based on the Larry McMurtry novel *Horseman, Pass By,* undercut or collapsed every optimistic assumption underlying *Red River* and *Giant.* In fact *Hud* is a kind of stripped-down version of both films. The John Wayne trail driver figure is replaced by Homer Bannon, an eighty-two-year-old stubborn, honest rancher who can remember trail drives of his youth. Only now he lives in a dying world. His cattle become infected with hoof-and-mouth disease and have to be exterminated. This is where the trail drives end, in a mass grave into which the cattle are driven, shot, and buried. Thus the *Red River* connection. From *Giant, Hud* borrows the iconography of the house, the patriarchal structure of the family, and the empty landscape. Only this time, the landscape is even bleaker, and the family is a grotesque parody in that the boy Lonnie has no father or mother, and the only loving maternal figure is the white housekeeper, Alma (Halmea in the novel) who is threatened with rape (in the film—in the novel, she is black and she is brutally raped). Hud is a version of Jett Rink in that he wants to drill for oil and will do whatever it takes to gain control of the land. Thus once again, the lust for quick wealth is at war with the pastoral virtues embodied in the older generation, just as in *Giant.* Paul Newman's charismatic portrayal of Hud dominates the film, and the audience's embrace of the anti-hero surprised director Martin Ritt: "It shocked me the first time I got a letter and it said that the old man is a pain in the ass and that Hud is right!" Larry McMurtry's comments on the making of the film, "Here's *Hud* in Your Eye," in his *In a Narrow Grave: Essays on Texas,* is a must-read.

Though *Hud* has been placed on the Preservation List, the current imprimateur of classic standing, it has some weaknesses that loom larger as the years pass. Despite Melvyn Douglas' winning an Academy Award for Best Supporting Actor, his portrayal of Homer Bannon seems unconvincing and un-Western. He is self-righteous to a fault and speaks in bumper-sticker moral slogans that become irritating. Equally weak is Brandon de Wilde's youth, Lonnie. He waddles like a duck when he walks and he too is sententious and boring once he casts his moral lot with his grandfather and turns against Hud. James Wong Howe's bleak, poetic black-and-white rendering of the landscape, for which he won an Academy Award for Cinematography, remains one of the most effective elements of the film, as is Patricia Neal's earthy portrayal of the housekeeper, Alma, for which she won an Oscar for Best Supporting Actress. ★

Hud (1963)
Courtesy Paramount

The Last Picture Show, 1971

It would seem that *Hud* would be the end of the line in the movement from expansive imperial optimism beginning with *Red River* and receiving its apotheosis in *Giant,* but in fact, the final coup de grâce to the Texas frontier/ cattleman myth appears in 1971's *The Last Picture Show,* also based on a McMurtry novel. The fact that two of the major Texas movies were drawn from Larry McMurtry novels adumbrates his importance in Texas literary and film culture, not to mention the award-winning film *Terms of Endearment* (1983) and the hit miniseries, *Lonesome Dove* (1994), also both deriving from McMurtry novels.

Like *Giant* and *Hud, The Last Picture Show* greatly benefits from being shot on location in West Texas, specifically in McMurtry's one stop-light home town, Archer City.

This is a Western without cowboys. The young boys in the film hope to work in the oil fields or see what's going on in Korea; they have no dreams of becoming cowboys or ranchers. The only character with any Western ties is Sam the Lion (Ben Johnson), who now lives (and dies) in the little town where he operates a pool hall and owns both the café and the movie theater. Sam the Lion used to be a rancher, but those days belong to a distant long ago that holds little interest for the current generation of oil men, oil drillers, and high school boys. Western movies are the only connection with that storied past.

The film is a very faithful adaptation of the novel. One difference, however, is that in the novel, instead of

The Last Picture Show (1971) Courtesy Columbia Pictures Industries, Inc.

roping steers, the boys date the local livestock. If sex in the film does not go quite this far, it goes pretty far. Sex is the preoccupation of most of the young people in the film, and the "old" have their innings too. Ruth Popper (Cloris Leachman), the coach's wife, takes Sonny (Timothy Bottoms) to bed, and Jacy Farrow's mother (Ellen Burstyn) is randier than any of the young girls, including her femme fatale daughter, Jacy (Cybill Shepherd). In fact, all the women characters are amazing, and one of the great strengths of the film is its ability to create fully drawn portraits of at least four women and a half dozen males. In all, *The Last Picture Show* racked up eight Academy Awards, including Best Picture. It became an instant classic, and unlike *Hud,* shows no signs of aging.)For those interested in the making of the film, there is a very good documentary directed by George Hickenlooper, *Picture This: The Times of Peter Bogdanovich in Archer City, Texas,*1991.)

  The Last Picture Show was an elegiac goodbye to the West, and a deeply pessimistic portrayal of the shoddy civilization created in its wake. In a moving nod to the great tradition, the last picture show to play at the Royal (the last picture show) is *Red River*. Bogdanovich shows an early, joyous scene from *Red River* as the cowboys set off on their epic journey up the long trail. In the novel the last movie is an Audie Murphy Western, *The Kid from Texas* (1950).

If *The Last Picture Show* was the end of a long line of big Texas Westerns, it was also the beginning of a long line of small Texas movies. We will come to those in due time. ★

The Wheeler Dealers, 1963

There is one more film to add to this sequence that runs from *Red River* to *The Last Picture Show*. The chronology takes us back to 1963 when Texans were still the Super-Americans and one of their own, Lyndon Johnson, was a heartbeat away from the presidency. Texans were larger than life, they were "long tall Texans" just like the song said, and they were often loveable as well. On Wednesday, November 20, 1963, *The Wheeler Dealers*, the best of the comic Texas movies, premiered in Dallas. For weeks leading up to its release the *Dallas Morning News* carried studio ads featuring Texas-brag jokes to create interest in the film. Texas-born Chill Wills was featured, along with jokes like this one: "Didja Hear the One about the Texan That Bought a Kid for His Dog?" Another ad appealed to local chauvinism: "If you're a born Texas (or even a transplanted one), you've gotta see us make fools of those Yankee New Yorkers."

Local Dallas film critic John Rosenfield defined the life cycle of a wheeler dealer for those unfamiliar with the term: On Sunday a man discovers oil on his farm, on Monday he moves to Dallas, on Tuesday he is elected president of the United Fund, on Wednesday he is chosen head of the Civic Opera, on Thursday he is made president of the Dallas Symphony, on Friday he is mentioned for U.S. Senator, on Saturday he learns that his acreage has a dry hole, and on Sunday he's back on the farm.

In *The Wheeler Dealers* the oilmen are cowboys, or dressed like cowboys gone to the city. James Garner, who plays the lead, Henry Tyroon (rhymes with tycoon), wears boots, a Western-cut suit, and string tie; and he drawls a lot. He is in fact an Easterner by birth and an Ivy Leaguer by education, with a major in Romance languages. Why the Texas persona? Because, says one character, "the best way to rub up against money was to be a Texan."

When Garner has several dry wells (in the film's opening scenes), he goes to New York to raise some cash to come back to Texas and drill some more wells. One of them is bound to hit; that's the wheeler-dealer's ethos. At one point he explains what he does when he loses money: "Well, then, I find some way for the, uh, government to take three-quarters of the loss."

Upon arriving in the Big Apple, he buys the taxi that picks him up at the airport, then he takes Molly Thatcher (Lee Remick), a pretty Wall Street broker to dine at a French restaurant where he orders his steak "burnt, with a mess of greens on the side." Later he buys the restaurant, and its snooty maître d' now has to bow and scrape before him.

The funniest wheeling and dealing in the movie comes when Garner and a simpering New York painter, Stanislas (played by Louis Nye), ransack Europe collecting Expressionist paintings as an experiment in venture capitalism. Showing off his hotel suite full of Kandinskys and the like, Garner brags, "Me and my boy Stan, we been wildcattin' all over the place." Later, Garner's three Texas cronies arrive, having flown their private jet to New York. They want a piece of the action and in very funny fashion use the jargon of oil transactions to talk about art: acreage, depletions, overrides. The three Texans, named Ray Jay (Phil Harris), Jay Ray (Chill Wills), and J. R. (Charles Watts), act as a comic chorus to Garner's more polished "Texan." They are in-color incarnations of Yell, Bragg, and Blow from *A Texas Steer*, just as Garner is an updated version of Will Rogers' Maverick Brander.

In the meantime Garner is still pursuing Lee Remick. She won't sleep with him, but she will marry him (just like in the Rock Hudson-Doris Day comedies of the late fifties). Garner's biggest financial venture in the East is a stock market scheme that fulfills his wheeler-dealer strategy: "I'm never illegal; just close to it." The whole thing is just for fun, he says: "Money's just the way you keep score." In *The Wheeler Dealers* money is style, a familiar and extravagant expression of exuberance and boundless optimism recognizable as the Texas version of the American dream. John Connally made much the same point in a more metaphysical way, in a quote attributed to him in James Conaway's *The Texans* (1976): "It's not a question of money, really. It's a question of *creativity*."

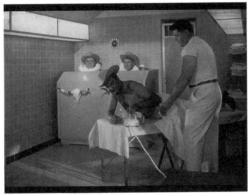

The Wheeler Dealers, 1963 Courtesy MGM.

The Wheeler Dealers played for two days before everything, in terms of the Texas image, changed. For on November 22, around high noon, another movie was being shot, this one on location, in downtown Dallas, in front of the School Book Depository Building. It was a kind of accidental minimalist Western. The "sheriff," the hero, JFK, with his jowly sidekick, LBJ, riding in the car behind, enters the frame of a homemade movie known to history as the Zapruder Film—313 frames long. They're riding into an ambush. There may be only one shooter—a loner, Lee Harvey Oswald—or a gang of multiple and never identified

43

or proven shooters on the grassy knoll; but the result is that the hero is dead within an hour.

So that day in Dallas, a *cinema vérité* was enacted in public view, in the streets. The next act took place two days later, and was part of a Western too. Another gunman attacked the accused assassin and killed him in full view of lawmen, one of whom was wearing a Stetson. What's missing from this composite real-life Western is the presence of a hero to prevent the twin miscarriages of justice. In the first instance, no steely-eyed horseman spotted the glint of the rifle in the bright sunshine of that autumn noon and pushed the intended target aside in the nick of time to save him, and in the second nobody among the assembled lawmen prevented the one-man lynch mob from accomplishing a second breach of justice.

Fifty-six feature films were playing in Dallas that week, and eight of them were Westerns. Two others were based on Texas stories, and of the ten films that were either Westerns or Texas-related, six had Texas associations. If you lived in Dallas, if you went to the movies, it was nearly impossible to escape the omnipresent Texas myth of gunplay, lawlessness, and frontier justice.

In the wake of the assassination, Texans portrayed in movies took a drubbing. In early 1964, Stanley Kubrick's *Dr. Strangelove* placed a Texan, Major King Kong, at the controls of the B-52 that is ordered to drop the H bomb on Russia. The last image of the film is Major Kong (Slim Pickens) waving his cowboy hat and giving a Texas cowboy whoop as he rides the bomb like a bucking bronc towards its target. In

Billion Dollar Brain (1967) based on a Len Deighton thriller, Ed Begley plays General Midwinter, a demented right-wing Texan who dresses in K-Mart leisure wear and has a war room "as big

Billion Dollar Brain (1967) Courtesy Tovera S.A.

*Dr. Strangelove, (*1964) Columbia; Courtesy Movie Star News.

as the Alamo" where he practices shooting at cut-out targets of Hitler and Stalin. The plot turns upon his paramilitary plan to overthrow a Communist satellite country in Scandinavia. *Executive Action* (1973), starring Burt Lancaster and Robert Ryan (in his last movie), had impeccable conspiracy credentials. Mark Lane, author of the first conspiracy book on the Kennedy assassination, *Rush to Judgment,* coauthored the story; Dalton Trumbo, the most famous of the Hollywood Ten, wrote the screenplay (his last such effort); and David Miller, another certified Hollywood liberal, directed. Its predicate of a right-wing conspiracy financed by a Texas billionaire was irresistible for those who wanted to blame

45

Dallas and real-life figures such as ultra rich oilman, H. L. Hunt. Years later, Oliver Stone would base his *JFK* (1991) on similar premises.

Two cultural moments marked a shift from the ugly Texan of the post-JFK assassination films to a return to an earlier tradition of mostly positive imagery: the TV show *Dallas,* which premiered in 1978, and the film *Urban Cowboy,* which appeared in 1980. *Dallas* made big money once again the definition of Texas, and *Urban Cowboy* ushered in the short-lived cultural phenomenon called Texas Chic. In the 1980s it was in TV that the big Texas stories—of oil wealth and cattle-drive heroics—were found now, not in the movies. *Dallas* and the hit miniseries *Lonesome Dove* (1994) were throwbacks to the days of the Super Americans in cinema.

A quick overview of Texas movies in the years since 1945 yields a couple of dozen worth detailed mention. Readers may easily supply their own lists, for film, more than any media, is a subjective parlor game. One's dogs are another's thoroughbreds, and so on. Among films not listed below are such contenders as *The Sugarland Express* (1974), *The Buddy Holly Story* (1978), *Alamo Bay* (1985), *Fandango* (1985), *Extreme Prejudice* (1987), *Talk Radio* (1988), *Slacker* (1991), *Love Field* (1992), A *Perfect World* (1993), *Flesh and Bone* (1993), *Apollo 13* (1995), The *Whole Wide World* (1996), *Tin Cup* (1996), and *Selena* (1997). ★

TEX MESSAGING
The Southerner, 1945

Famed French director Jean Renoir (*Grand Illusion*, 1937, *The Rules of the Game*, 1939) spent World War II in Hollywood, where he directed three American films. The best of them was *The Southerner* (1945), based on George Sessions Perry's *Hold Autumn in Your Hand*, the most compelling novel about farm life ever written by a Texan. Renoir wrote the script, along with Hugo Butler, and an uncredited William Faulkner. Renoir wanted to shoot the film on Perry's home ground, in and around Rockdale, sixty miles northeast of Austin, but in the end it was filmed in Southern California. Like the novel, the film explores the economic conditions of tenant farming at the tag end of the Depression, around 1940. Some scenes of picking and weighing cotton carry an authentic flavor. Drawing upon his sympathy for French pastoral virtues, Renoir is able to create a mostly affecting portrait of American peasants (though

The Southerner (1945)
Courtesy Jean Renoir
Productions.

47

they would not like being called that) struggling to survive.

Besides the erasure of East Texas in *The Southerner*, there is a good deal of broad comedy that doesn't play well today. Percy Kilbride, who played Pa Kettle in the Ma-and-Pa Kettle comedy series, brings his Maine accent to East Texas, with unintentionally laughable results.

But the story of Sam Tucker (Zachary Scott) and his wife Nona (Betty Field) is quite watchable, although Scott, a native Texan, is a bit too urbane to be entirely convincing as a dirt-poor working man. His wife, described in the novel as a "blank," is transformed in the film into a cigarette-smoking blonde who wears designer jeans and seems to belong in somebody's drawing room rather than a run-down shack. A cranky grandmother, two children, and a bad neighbor round out the major characters. *The Southerner* was awarded "Best of Festival" at the 1946 Venice Film Festival and picked as Number Three of the "Ten Best Films of the Year" by the National Board of Review. It also received three Academy Award nominations, one for Sound, one for Scoring of a Dramatic Picture, and one for Best Director.

The Southerner, in its displacement of Texas into the generic South, is typical of what happens with movies ostensibly set in East Texas. The specific sense of an East Texas landscape and topography is lost. Such films routinely either translate East Texas pines into West Texas cactus, or blur East Texas into the Old South, and in either case the sense of East Texas is lost. Examples are plentiful. In *American Empire* (1942) the action takes place on a ranch near the Sabine River, on the border between Texas and

Louisiana. Yet snow-clad mountains loom in the middle distance. In *All the Fine Young Cannibals* (1960), a train leaving Dallas for New York passes through what appears to be an Arizona desert. In *A Walk on the Wild Side* (1962) a sign reading "Beaumont—One Mile" stands in the middle of a desert with tumbleweeds rolling past. In *4 for Texas* (1963) Galveston is a Western town with snow-clad mountains near by. In *Missing in Action* (1983), a scene depicting high mountains and a valley far below is identified with the words "North of Galveston." Almost all movies said to be set in East Texas are not.

And there is the occasional anomaly: a West Texas story filmed in East Texas. Such is the heartbreak of *Lovin' Molly* (1974), based on Larry McMurtry's second novel, *Leaving Cheyenne,* and directed by Sidney Lumet who had apparently never traveled beyond Manhattan. Filmed in the Bastrop area, the film gets everything wrong. Tony Perkins plays a cowboy who wears L.L. Bean shirts (over a black Tee shirt) and flat-soled shoes; he looks ridiculous. But no more so than Blythe Danner, the Molly of the title, an earth-mother who clasps a freshly born calf, still wet with after-birth, to her bosom. Amazing. *Variety* called the

Lovin' Molly (1974)
Courtesy Columbia.

49

film "misguided" and "heavy handed," which was putting it mildly. McMurtry himself wrote a wonderful essay titled "Leaving Lumet," about how wrong-headed this film is. Its chief competitor as the worst Texas movie ever is Robert Altman's *Dr. T and the Women* (2000), a late excursion into Texas movie madness. In this film by the vastly overrated director, Dallas is the site of big-haired rich women who worship a gynecologist played by the great Texas actor Richard Gere. They adore him, and in his waiting room, a place in real life of real angst, they cluck and chatter like a barnyard full of simpering hens. The feminists who hated this movie were right; it is deeply misogynist no matter what critics like Roger Ebert say. ★

Lucy Gallant, 1955

Originally titled "Oil Town," this film introduced a whole new theme to Texas films—the fashion show à la Neiman-Marcus. The time is the 1950s. Charlton Heston plays stalwart West Texas rancher Casey Cole and Jane Wyman plays Lucy Gallant, a single woman who moves to a small, dusty West Texas town where she hopes to carve out a living for herself. Heston pursues her the whole movie, while she builds up a mercantile empire on her own. Before oil was discovered (in the Midland area, one assumes), women dressed dowdily (as they do in *Giant*), but after oil makes all the landowners rich, the women need somewhere upmarket to shop. Enter Lucy Gallant with her new high couture department store. Instead of buying dresses off the rack at J. C. Penney's, now the wives can spend all day at viewings, style shows, and fittings. At one of the shows, gorgeous models, flown in from somewhere, parade around as though they were in Milan. Of special interest in this scene is the appearance of Governor Allen Shivers, who sits beside Lucy Gallant during the high fashion extravaganza.

Heston is very good, in that macho way he had, but Lucy Gallant's decision to give up her business career and marry him at the end, may seem too "Fifties" for a lot of career women today. Sociologically, this film remains interesting for its portrait of the impact that oil and sudden wealth had on provincial West Texas towns. ★

The Searchers, 1956

One of the most important movies in American cinema history, *The Searchers* has been credited with influencing such films as *Taxi Driver* (1976), *The Deer Hunter* (1978), *Hard*

Core (1979), *Paris, Texas* (1984), and *The Missing* (2003), among others. The story line follows one of the oldest American genres, the captivity narrative, which goes all the way back to Colonial America. Typically, an Anglo woman is captured by Indians, and the plot turns upon the attempt to rescue and return her to family and community. In Texas, the most famous instance of captivity and return was that of Cynthia Ann Parker, and it is her story that underpins both the Alan Le May novel on which the film was based and the film itself.

The Searchers is celebrated for many other reasons. First is its combination of director and star: John Ford and John Wayne. Ford used his favorite place, Monument Valley, to represent West Texas, and every critic has admired the beauty of the landscape shots. He also uses his favorite actor, John Wayne, to powerful effect. In Wayne's most memorable films—*Red River, The Sands of Iwo Jima* (1949), and *The Searchers*—he is best when he goes a little bit crazy, when his iron will pushes him beyond the limits of ordinary human behavior and he becomes obsessed with imposing his view of the world. In *The Searchers* Wayne's hatred of Indians drives him to seek his niece Debbie (Natalie Wood), who has been stolen by the Comanches and who, he fears, has become the "bride" of a Comanche chief—as indeed it turns out.

For ten years Ethan Edwards (Wayne) pursues his lost niece, and the audience comes to believe that when he finds her, he will kill her for the "sin" of miscegenation. Jean Luc-Godard, the French *auteur*, has spoken memorably of the famous moment in the film when Wayne is reunited

The Searchers (1956) Courtesy Warner Bros.

with his niece: "How can I hate John Wayne upholding Goldwater and yet love him tenderly when abruptly he takes Natalie Wood into his arms in the last reel of *The Searchers?*" The answer is Wayne's kinetic acting, the surge and grace of his body as he sweeps her up from the ground and comforts her. The metaphysics of family, race, and national destiny have rarely been portrayed as powerfully in American film.

There are weaknesses, however. The score, imposed by Warner Bros., prevented Ford from relying on period music as he does in films like *My Darling Clementine* (1946). As a result, in *The Searchers* there is no singing of great, evocative songs like "Shall We Gather at the River." There is also too much broad comedy, and a ridiculous side-plot with an Indian woman named Look who tags along following Wayne and his youthful sidekick, Martin Pawley (Jeffrey Hunter).

For all of the tributes to this film, its influence upon other directors, its lofty standing among critics, it is as solemn at that other much talked-about classic, *Citizen Kane* (1941), and sometimes, just as boring. ★

53

Written on the Wind, 1956

Here is Texas in a sudsy mode, an over-the-top melodrama that some film critics—Roger Ebert, for instance—regard as a great movie. The story line deals with a filthy-rich oil family living in Texas. The patriarch has two very troubled children: Kyle Hadley (Robert Stack) and Marylee Hadley (Dorothy Malone). Both were nominated for Academy Awards for Supporting Actor and Actress, and Malone won. Both play their roles with a level of hysteria that causes the viewer either to marvel at their neuroses or to laugh. The whole movie walks the borderline between melodrama and camp parody. Kyle is a nearly impotent alcoholic, and Marylee is an accomplished nymphomaniac. The object of Marylee's eye is Mitch Wayne, a macho Texan whose name is probably a play on those two movie paragons of manliness,

Written on the Wind (1956) Universal-International;
Courtesy Wisconsin Center for Film and Theater.

Robert Mitchum and John Wayne. Rock Hudson plays Mitch Wayne—more insider comedy? Kyle is terribly jealous of Hudson's sturdy integrity and manliness. Kyle and Marylee are the way they are because they grew up spoiled rotten by great wealth, and Mitch Wayne is the way he is—a pillar of ethical earnestness—because he grew up poor, on the Hadley ranch with the Hadley kids.

Director Douglas Sirk wrings every ounce of soap opera emotion he can from the main four characters (the fourth is a too old Lauren Bacall being the love object of Kyle, whom she throws over for a piece of the Rock). Sirk was a German who spent his first thirty-seven years working as a stage-director in Germany before coming to Hollywood to escape Hitler's Reich. In the 1950s he made a series of lush melodramas including *Magnificent Obsession* (1954) and *Imitation of Life* (1959). *Written on the Wind* shares with them a love of opulence, the use of artificial sets and backdrops to signify the emptiness of American materialism, and a full deck of dysfunctional obsessions of the kind that would later fuel TV soaps like *Dallas* and *Dynasty*.

At the end of the film, bereft of Mitch Wayne, and alone with her empire (her father and brother are both dead), Marylee sits at her father's desk in the main office of Hadley Oil Co. and clutches a very phallic model oil derrick that adorns the desk. With Sirk, whatever was obvious was art.

The film can be seen in a knowing, cinematic way or as pastiche and parody, but it cannot be taken seriously as realistic drama. Nor should it be seen twice. Once is enough. ★

The Alamo, 1960

The Alamo (1960) Courtesy The Library of
the Daughters of the Republic of Texas at the Alamo.

This lengthy epic cost $12 million in 1959, setting a short-lived record as the most expensive film in movie history up to that point. It was shot on location in Texas, just outside of Bracketville, on Happy Shahan's ranch where a false-front Alamo was constructed, along with a "Western" town. Over the years many Westerns were helmed there.

John Wayne directed, and although he didn't want to play a role himself, he had to in order to secure financial backing. His Crockett is a man whose motives are summed up in a boiler-plate speech authored by screenwriter James Edward Grant: "Republic, I like the sound of the word. It means people can live free, talk free, go or come, be drunk or sober, however they choose . . ." yada, yada, yada. Laurence Harvey lends a priggish air to Colonel Travis, and Richard Widmark plays a prickly Jim Bowie. (Widmark's off-screen rudeness to Wayne has been much remarked on.) The film is overly long (167 minutes) but has its moments. One of them is the way Wayne stages the decisive moment when Travis asks the men to decide whether they are going to stay and die, or not. In most films, following the legend, Travis draws a line in the sand, but in Wayne's world Travis addresses the crowd of men while Crockett and Bowie, on horseback, dismount to join the other men standing on the ground. Thus the drama of democratic equality and solidarity is effectively expressed.

Despite repeated claims of a desire to achieve historical accuracy, *The Alamo* starts with a laugher when Richard Boone's Sam Houston tells Travis and company that "You people, you people right here on the Rio Grande, are going to have to buy me that time." The problem is that they weren't on the Rio Grande, which is nearly two hundred miles from San Antonio; they were on the San Antonio River, two blocks from the old mission. The other error here is that Houston's orders were to burn the Alamo, not defend it.

The assault on the Alamo is handled well, but doesn't occur until thirty minutes from the end. Wayne's Crockett dies blowing up a powder keg, a pretty good way for Crockett to go out, with a bang.

John Wayne had it right, though, even if his film didn't, when he called the Alamo story "the greatest piece of folklore ever brought down through history, and folklore has always been the most successful medium for motion pictures."

The film won one Oscar, for Sound. ★

The Unforgiven, 1960

This John Huston Western, filmed in Durango, Mexico, featured an all-star cast, including Burt Lancaster, Audrey Hepburn, and Lillian Gish. During location shooting, Hepburn broke her back, and Audie Murphy nearly drowned in a near-by lake. Like *The Searchers*, this film too was based on an Alan Le May novel, and it shares some of the racial anxieties and tensions of the more famous John Ford film. The story line concerns the identity of a young woman, Rachael Zachary (Hepburn) who has been raised in a boisterous frontier family headed by Ben Zachary (Lancaster). In one of the best roles of his career, Murphy, sporting a mustache, is terrific as Cash Zachary, a hot-headed, Indian-hating brother to Ben, who appears to have more than brotherly feelings for the adopted Rachel.

Everything gets very tense as rumors abound that Rachel is actually of Kiowa blood, and the Kiowas come to claim her in a series of raids on the Zachary cabin. In one of the most memorable scenes, Mattilda Zachary (Gish), the matriarch, plays a piano placed outside the thatched sod cabin, in the bright sunlight; later the Kiowas, no respecters of high culture, pepper the piano with their arrows. At times hysterical and at times compelling, *The Unforgiven* continues to draw a wide range of responses from viewers. Huston himself claimed that this film was the only one of his that he did not like, but when one remembers that he also directed *Moby Dick* (1956), his distancing himself from *The Unforgiven* does not seem to carry so much weight. ★

The Unforgiven (1960) Courtesy James Productions.

Bonnie and Clyde, 1967

Perhaps it's no accident that the two most violent and revolutionary films of the 1960s were set in Texas. The first was *Bonnie and Clyde,* and it now seems much less of a cinema milestone than the second, *The Wild Bunch* (1969). The best things about *Bonnie and Clyde* are the authentic flavor of the 1930s achieved by location shooting in small towns in North Texas and by expert period costuming. Some scenes seem to come right out of the Depression era: Bonnie's mother beside a camp fire, a black sharecropper firing Clyde Barrow's pistol at a bank's foreclosure sign, the little country dry goods stores, the old Ford automobiles of the kind that Clyde loved.

But what has not worn so well is the two principals, considerably duded up from the original pair of outlaws. Beatty is consistently annoying, mainly because he is so in

59

love with himself; and the idea of playing a character with erectile dysfunction, which reviewers at the time felt was daring, now seems like a smirk-a-minute bit of onanistic self-congratulation. The violence is tonally both rousing and irritating because of the incessant Flatt and Scruggs bluegrass sound track that accompanies the Tommie-gun sequences. One can see how stylish and avant-garde the film seemed in 1967, but much of that energy seems now to be rhetorically empty; the film is about nothing except Beatty's ego. One thing that hasn't aged is Gene Hackman's take on Clyde's brother, Buck. It's a wonderful bit of naturalistic acting that makes Beatty's mannered self-absorption seem pale by comparison. ★

Bonnie and Clyde (1969)
Courtesy Warner
Bros.-Seven Arts.

The Wild Bunch (1969)
Courtesy Warner Brothers.

The Wild Bunch, 1969

The closest the Western has come to creating tragic emotions, this ultraviolent film is Sam Peckinpah's masterpiece. It begins and ends with a massacre. The opening sequence, a slaughter of the innocents in a little South Texas border town named San Rafael, precipitates the outlaw gang's flight into *"Mexico lindo,"* which, as one gang member says, "just looks like more Texas." But it isn't; it's 1913 and there's a revolution going on and the bunch figures to play both sides against the middle. Although the Texas ambience in the film is thin (only the opening sequence is set there), the film manages to create a better sense of a "last stand" than any of the Alamo movies do.

Once in Mexico, pursued by a ragged, mad-dog band of bounty-hunters, the gang finds succor in the village of one of their members, Angel, the purest of the bunch. The scene of departure from Angel's village is one of the most beautiful sequences in American film. As the men ride beneath the trees and doff their hats at the assembled villagers, the song "La Golondrina" plays in the background. As Peckinpah later said of the outlaw gang in this scene: "If you can ride with them there and feel it, you can die with them and feel it."

Pike Bishop (William Holden in his greatest role) knows that the old days are "closing fast." New weapons—machine guns—and new forms of transportation—automobiles and airplanes—signal a new world and a new war just over the horizon in Europe. At Agua Verde, a town held in the grip of a vicious alliance between General Mapache and some German "advisors," Pike and his men contract to steal weapons from the U.S. Army. In the process he and his men sacrifice Angel (Jaime Sanchez) to the tyrant Mapache. Pike's words that launch the famous walk into the courtyard to rescue Angel consist of one short sentence, "Let's go," followed by Warren Oates' "Why not?" The final Gotterdammerung is incredibly powerful. In frame after frame Peckinpah brings out the pathos of the end of an era. It is also a film about honor, one of the old standby themes of the Western, but never done with more complexity or beauty or emotion than in this film. Editing, composition, music, acting, directing, are all superb. Paul Seydor's documentary about the making of the film, *The Wild Bunch: An Album in Montage* (1996), is highly recommended, as is David Weddle's book on Peckinpah, *If They Move . . . Kill 'Em!* ★

The Getaway, 1972

In this crime caper film directed by Sam Peckinpah, Texas locations are evident throughout: San Marcos, San Antonio, El Paso. Steve McQueen plays a professional criminal named Doc McCoy who, when the film opens, is just coming out of stir to join his girlfriend, Carol (Ali McGraw, who famously became McQueen's girlfriend during the making of the film). He wants to rob one last bank and escape to Mexico, and he and Carol pull it off, but not without a lot of bloodletting and car chases before they are done. The supporting cast includes the always reliable Ben Johnson, playing a crooked law man; and Al Lettiere as a crude, brutal, and sadistic criminal who pursues McCoy and his moll to get the stolen money.

McQueen wears a dark suit with an open-collar white shirt and looks great all the way through the film. The film is packed with memorable sequences, including a long chase-in-a-train that is worthy of Hitchcock.

A shoot-out in a seedy El Paso hotel is one of the best gunplay sequences that has ever been filmed. McQueen handles a pump shot-gun like nobody else.

Peckinpah knew he was just making a genre film and didn't expend his usual amount of angst over it. The film made money, too. It remains very watchable. ★

The Getaway (1969)
National General. Photo
courtesy Texas Film
Commission.

Days of Heaven (1978)
Courtesy Paramount
Pictures.

Days of Heaven, 1978

Terrence Malick, a native Texan who has built up a substantial reputation on the basis of a small number of films, has dealt with his home state in only one. In *Days of Heaven* the Panhandle setting is beautiful, and why shouldn't it be since the film was shot in Alberta, Canada. Anytime cinematography receives top billing in reviews, that usually means there's trouble elsewhere in the film.

It comes in the glacial pace of the film, and in one of the central figures, a very young Richard Gere. Gere simply never looks like a working-class youth on the lam from trouble in a steel mill near Chicago, where the film opens. He and his girlfriend (Brooke Adams), who, for reasons unknown, poses as his sister, and his younger sister come to the "Texas Panhandle" to work in the wheat fields sometime before World War I.

The best thing in the film, besides the pretty pictures, is the ironic, hard-boiled narration of the younger sister, played by Linda Manz. Her voice has a world-weary quality about it, as though, even at a very young age, she has seen just how sad and dangerous the world can be. At one point the three of them are in a boat on a river, and she says, "You could see people on the shore, but it was far off and you couldn't see what they were doing. They were probably calling for help or something—or they were trying to bury somebody or something." She might have been reading lines from Stephen Crane's "The Open Boat." ★

North Dallas Forty. 1979

This is a fine adaptation of Peter Gent's ahead-of-its-time *roman à clef* about the Dallas Cowboys during the Don Meredith-Tom Landry era. Wrongly classified as "comedy" in most video stores, *North Dallas Forty* examines the darker side of professional football. Mac Davis, a West Texan, gives a credible performance as a fun-loving quarterback, and his antics may be where the comedy label comes in.

Like the novel, the film exposes a win-at-any-cost mentality of coaches and owners. Not that this is news to anybody today, but it was in the 1970s. The premise is that football players are no different from blue-collar workers in an industrial factory; their sole purpose is to produce league titles. B.A. Strothers (G.D. Spradlin), the Landry-like coach, is a play-it-by-the-computer automaton who overlooks his stars' off-field behavior but discards lesser players for the same misbehavior.

Drug use to overcome real physical pain blurs into continuous recreational use, and nobody cares as long as the players win on Sunday. Team doctors routinely hand out drugs to keep injured players in the line-up. Phil Elliot (expertly played by Nick Nolte) is a talented but rebellious wide receiver (much like author Peter Gent) who calls the callous drug policy "better football through better chemistry." In the end Elliot proves expendable and is cut from the team. He has something to fall back on, a small ranch where he hopes to raise horses and live with his girlfriend.

This is one of the best football movies ever made and far superior to two more recent films about high school football: *Varsity Blues* (1999) and *Friday Night Lights* (2004). ★

North Dallas Forty (1979) Courtesy of Paramount.

Urban Cowboy, 1980

This film, which made Texas fashions the new thing for about six months, probably should have been titled "Suburban Cowboy," since its principal setting is the Houston working-class suburb of Pasadena. Here stood the famous Gilley's where would-be cowboys and cowboyettes came to dance the two-step, drink Lone Star beer, and ride mechanical bulls. It was a cultural moment of short duration, and Texas author Aaron Latham (married to TV's Leslie Stahl) recognized, in a visit to Gilley's in 1978, that there was something interesting going on. His article in *Esquire* captured the scene perfectly, and the film got much of the article right.

John Travolta, dressed like Tom Mix from the 1920s, in jeans, pearl-studded shirt, and cowboy hat, has to leave his native acres, in Spur (Latham's West Texas home town) and move to Houston/Pasadena where he goes to work in the petrochemical business. The work is dangerous, and the main relief from those hard-hat days is to go country-western dancing at Gilley's. There he meets the most compelling figure in the movie, Sissie, played with great authenticity by Debra Winger. Sissie is from a blue-collar background too and has a job driving a wrecker that picks up cars smashed up on the Houston freeways. They get married at Gilley's and they live in a mobile home where the dishes and laundry pile up because they are too busy working and going to Gilley's to take care of such mundane tasks.

The weakest part of the movie is the plot: a villain borrowed from Western movies, played by Scott Glenn, sets a tequila-laced trap to seduce Sissie, while Bud (Travolta) has a fling with a rich cowgirl. The other weak part is the music. It's not really country-western music, it's not Merle Haggard or George Jones. "Looking for Love in All the Wrong Places," the most popular hit from the film, is not a country-western song, at least not in any meaningful sense. As proof, here is a comment from a "reviewer" on the IMDB site: "The sound track was dynamite (and this comes from a guy who can't stand the sound of country music)." That's because there is no country music in this film.

Deborah Winger is great, and she's the main reason to see this film. Once. ★

Urban Cowboy (1980)
Courtesy Paramount
Pictures.

Middleage Crazy, 1980

Co-written by legendary songbird Jerry Lee Lewis, this is the story of an aging urban cowboy. Bobby Lee (Bruce Dern) is turning forty and he's not happy about it. He has to take care of his aging mother, a son who wants to drop out of college, and his sexy wife (Ann-Margret) who expects him to be the same stud he used to be. Bobby Lee is a contractor who, among other things, builds taco stands in Houston, but when he gets a job in Dallas remodeling a box at Texas Stadium, he cuts loose from all the ties that bind. He buys a Porsche, starts wearing urban cowboy regalia, and falls head-over-cowboy heels for a Dallas Cowboys Cheerleader.

In retaliation, his wife has a fling, and everything in his life is imperiled. The film is pretty good until he recovers from his desire for another life, and everything turns warm and fuzzy as he reconciles with his wife and family. By the end the sense of an authentic film has yielded to the boring contentment of a made-for-TV problem movie.

There's one great scene, though, when Bobby Lee, fully dressed, is on the bed with Ann-Margret, fully dressed, and he seems puzzled about what to do next. This is the ultimate pre-Viagra moment in Texas movies, and one of the few films in which Bruce Dern does not play a deranged character. Dern and Ann-Margret are quite good at capturing the lives of a down-home couple caught up in a nouveau-riche lifestyle. ★

Middle Age Crazy (1983)
Courtesy Canadian Film
Development Corporation.

Hard Country (1981)
Courtesy Universal.

Hard Country, 1981

Overshadowed by *Urban Cowboy*, this film, based on a song by cosmic cowboy Michael Martin Murphey, explores the tensions between a smart, ambitious young woman living in West Texas and her loutish, culture-bound boyfriend. Jodie (Kim Basinger, in her film debut) works at a telephone company but dreams of something better. Kyle (Jan-Michael Vincent), her boyfriend, works at a chain-link fence factory named Prairie Fence Company. The don't-fence-me-in motif is thus rather obviously present. Like the young couple in *Urban Cowboy*, Jodie and Kyle spend their evenings at a honky-tonk, the Stallion, a knock-off of Gilley's. There Kyle and his buddies chug-a-lug beers and generally act obnoxiously, while Jodie dutifully watches but longs for elsewhere.

Elsewhere is the life led by singing star Carole, played by Tanya Tucker. She's from the same town and comes back from her glamorous life in L.A. to visit her old friends, along with her Gucci-wearing L.A. boyfriend who receives some stupid redneck harassment from Kyle and his fellow cowboys. Tucker delivers the key lines of the film when she explains to Jodie, "A woman who needs space for herself gets out of Texas. It's a great place to be from and a great place to come home to but you've gotta leave it first, before it smothers her." The film slows down when Tucker sings, as she does at least one more time than is needed.

At the end Jodie leaves for L.A. where she has a good job opportunity as a flight attendant with "Western

Airlines." She gets on the plane and is ready to fly away when along comes Kyle, dressed in his usual shitkicker attire. Kyle has decided that his love for her is stronger than his attachment to Texas. In what seems like a big mistake, she agrees to take him with her to California. He will need to get some new duds or the L.A. crowd is going to laugh him back to Texas. ★

The Border, 1982

In this modern Western Jack Nicholson acted for one of the last times before he started mailing in cartoonish caricatures of himself. He plays an honest Border Patrol agent named Charley Smith, who gets transferred from California to El Paso. The drama of his efforts to resist temptation is the center of the film. His tempters include Harvey Keitel, an engaging good ol' boy on the take, and Valerie Perrine, Charley's sexy, gum-chewing, K-Mart decked-out wife who longs to be a Dallas Cowboys Cheerleader and spends every penny he doesn't make, buying waterbeds and tacky sofas on credit. Warren Oates, who is always superb, plays Charley's corrupt boss. One of the script writers was Walon Green, who worked on *The Wild Bunch.* Green knows this kind of world and is very adept at capturing it. The film was shot in Antigua, Guatemala, but the viewer always thinks it's El Paso.

Although Charley reluctantly accepts the skewed ethics of an everybody-does-it system that preys on the dreams of illegal aliens seeking to come to America, he eventually achieves redemption when he takes up the cause of a lovely Mexican Madonna whose baby is stolen by an adoption ring. Though the plot device of the world-weary law officer being softened by a mother-and-baby is as old as William S. Hart's Westerns, there is enough fast-paced action and hard-bitten atmospherics to disguise the number being done on the viewer's emotions. But most of all there is Nicholson's stubborn, convincing refusal to give up on his fundamental decency.

One minus in the film is there are so many night scenes that unless the copy is perfect, the viewing is most decidedly not. One big plus is Ry Cooder's soundtrack, featuring the great song "Across the Borderline," sung movingly by Freddie Fender.

This gritty, realistic movie was Englishman Tony Richardson's last film. ★

The Border (1983) Courtesy Efer Productions.

Terms of Endearment, 1983

Shot in Houston, this film turns the Bayou City into a coastal suburbia, but the real interest lies in the dynamics of a terrific, till-death-do-us-part relationship between an imperious mother, Aurora Greenway (Shirley MacLaine), and her sweet, affecting daughter, Emma, played beautifully by Debra Winger. Jack Nicholson, a randy retired astronauat thrown in to liven up the neighborhood, brings some over-the-top comic lust into the film.

The movie is much thinner in Texas ambience than the Larry McMurtry novel on which it was based, and quite possibly the better for it.

Emma's marriage to unfaithful academic loser Flap Horton (Jeff Daniels) is another strong strand in the film. But her harrowing death from cancer makes everything else seem irrelevant. The bedside scenes in the cancer ward would wring tears from a serial killer. It is a far superior mother-daughter film than that other weepy favorite of the 1980s, *Steel Magnolias* (1989). *Terms of Endearment* won Five Oscars, including Best Picture and Best Director (James Brooks). Years later, *Entertainment Weekly* rated it the top tear-jerker of all time.

The sequel, *The Evening Star,* based on McMurtry's novel of the same title, appeared in 1997. Shirley MacLaine resurrects Aurora Greenway, and Jack Nicholson puts in a cameo appearance, but all the pathos and sharp characterizations of the first film are missing from this lackluster effort. Only the lonely would like this one. ★

Tender Mercies, 1983

This is the best of Horton Foote's numerous essays in Texas filmmaking, including the overrated *Trip to Bountiful* (1985) or the underrated *1918* (1985). This quiet study of a country and western singer on the skids has an authentic, unforced feel to it that is welcome in a story about lives as plain as hillbilly ballads. Australian director Bruce Beresford, who made the great historical film *Breaker Morant* (1980), brings a sure eye to the characters and the landscape near Waxahachie, Texas.

Robert Duvall, who won the Academy Award for Best Actor for this role, is perfect as Mac Sledge, both in his Depression-inflected, stoic acceptance of life's hard knocks, and his twangy accent, the best rendition of East Texas speech ever recorded in a feature film. Duvall is also a very good country western singer and does a far better job of impersonating a country singer than stars such as Dolly Parton, Willie Nelson, and Kris Kristoffersen have done in their various boring movies about songwriters, madams, and whatever. Tess Harper is also good in a stand-by-your-man role typical of the culture being dramatized.

Finally, this film manages to treat rural Protestantism with a degree of honesty very rare in American films. Mac Sledge is baptized in church, not in a river, and every detail and emotion is right—very unusual. ★

The Ballad of Gregorio Cortez, 1983

Based on Américo Paredes' *"With His Pistol in His Hand:" A Border Ballad and Its Hero,* this film tells the story of Mexican-American folk hero, Gregorio Cortez. In 1901 Cortez shot a deputy as the result of a misunderstanding over ownership of a horse. Fearing a lynch mob, Cortez fled his home near Gonzales, Texas, east of San Antonio, and headed for the Mexican border. The chase lasted eleven days, covered 450 miles, and involved a posse of 600 men led by Texas Rangers. By means of more gunplay and skilled horsemanship, Cortez managed to elude the lawmen and armed citizens and make his way to the border, where he was betrayed by a Mexican-American and brought back for trial. The case created a sensation in Texas, and Cortez became the hero of *corridos,* or border ballads, songs sung along the border and in the brush country of South Texas that celebrated his courage and cleverness while mocking the greed and stupidity of the hated *rinches* (Rangers).

Cortez served twelve years of a fifty-year sentence before receiving a gubernatorial pardon.

Edward James Olmos lends a quiet dignity to Cortez, though the film never generates imaginative power to match its good intentions. The film needed better production values and a stronger supporting cast. Some of the acting feels amateurish at times. Nonetheless, it enjoyed considerable popularity outside the U.S. It is too bad that this film did not inspire other revisionist cinema that would explore Texas history from the Mexican-American perspective, particularly in South Texas where the Anglo version of Texas history is still contested. ★

The Ballad of Gregorio Cortez (1983) Courtesy Embassy Pictures Corporation.

Blood Simple, 1984

A honky-tonk film noir shot in Austin on a modest budget, this first film by Joel and Ethan Coen still ranks as one of the best in their considerable oeuvre. And it is certainly the best noir film ever set in Texas. The story line involves two lovers (John Getz and Frances McDormand, in her movie debut), a jealous husband (Dan Hedaya) who wants them dead, and most memorable of all, a sleazy detective played beautifully by M. Emmet Walsh.

The opening narration sets the tone. The detective, who drives a beat-up old VW bug, intones, "In Russia they got it mapped out, so that everyone pulls for everyone else.

That's the theory, anyway. But what I know about is Texas, and down here you're on your own."

This film reinvigorates the noir genre by adding some standard-issue gothic touches: scary camera angles, the corpse that won't die, a knife in the hand, etc. *Blood Simple* is a dark delight from beginning to end. ★

Flashpoint, 1984

In this underrated and overlooked film, two hardworking border patrol agents (Kris Kristofferson and Treat Williams) keep finding things in the desert in southwest Texas that get them in trouble. They unearth a drug-smuggling operation, then two friendly young women asleep in a car, and finally and most importantly, a buried jeep that contains a sniper's rifle, a driver's license and other papers all dated 1962–1963, and $800,000 in cash. Kristofferson's worldly character is in favor of splitting the money and vanishing, but Williams, more idealistic, wants to find out where it came from. This leads them to investigate clues that the viewer picks up on before they do, and soon they realize that what they have discovered is a rifle used in the Kennedy assassination.

They never do find out the identity of the shooter, however. Washington-based bureaucrats in suits are the biggest enemies of all, and the film moves towards a satisfactorily bloody conclusion with one partner dead and one alive on his way to Mexico with the money. The photography is excellent, and Kristofferson's performance is especially strong.

There is one funny moment when the two agents drive to what is supposed to be "San Antonio" and enter what is obviously an Arizona city—a desert-town surrounded by mountains. ★

Places in the Heart, 1984

Written and directed by native Texan Robert Benton, this mortgage melodrama is set in the area where he grew up, in Waxahachie and environs, around 1935. It is nostalgic, with lots of pretty cinematography reminiscent of Depression-era documentary; overly ambitious; and crowded with too many characters and subplots. Even the main story seems improbable at times. Sally Fields plays a widow who goes into the cotton-farming business with the help of a black ex-sharecropper (Danny Glover) and a blind man (John Malkovich). Already this is too much. Fields is a quick learner, and the first thing you know, she's in a field dwarfed by gigantic cotton plants. But any attempt to make picking cotton dramatic is doomed to failure. Picking cotton is stoop labor, emphasis on stoop and labor.

The film covers a one-year cycle of planting and picking, and during that time a tornado swoops down on the farm and the KKK makes an appearance to drive home the racism of the era. But Field and her children and her helpers overcome the cruelty of both nature and man. The closing scene is a fantasy in which black and white, friends and enemies, the living and the dead are all joined together in a church communion service. It's a Big Ending, and for some viewers it's really wonderful, and for others it's manipulative and sentimental.

Benton won an Oscar for Best Original Screenplay and Fields for Best Actress. ★

Lone Star, 1996

John Sayles wrote and directed this highly praised, ambitious attempt to take the pulse of modern Texas. Roger Ebert, for example, calls it a "great American film," but Barbara Shufgasser of the *San Francisco Examiner* is much closer to the mark when she says that although Sayles' intentions and humanism are admirable, sitting through the movie "is often a chore." It's the kind of film that lends itself to academic analysis but it's not a great cinematic experience. The main problem is that Sayles tries to get too much material into one film. Set in a Texas border town, the imaginary Frontera, the film is crowded with multicultural groups including Tejanos, African Americans, Anglo Texans, and Black Seminoles. Into this mix Sayles weaves stories dealing with racism, illegal immigrants, murder, incest, interracial relationships, and discourse on how Texas history should be taught.

The film's best story line involves the attempts by Sheriff Sam Deeds (Chris Cooper) to solve a murder when a body is found in the desert that is the remains of a former (and savagely racist) sheriff played menacingly by Kris Krisofferson in flashback scenes. This search into Frontera's troubled past leads him to reunite with a childhood sweetheart, Pilar (Elizabeth Pena), who he learns is his half-sister. They fall in love again and plan to be married but will not, we are assured, have children. Pilar is a history teacher, and in one exchange with Sam, which occurs appropriately in an abandoned, dilapidated drive-in movie, the site of Texas mythology, she says the words that best capture the spirit of the film: "Forget the Alamo." The original words in the script used another F word but the line was changed. (Sayles himself did not forget the Alamo however, for a few years later he wrote a long script on the Alamo that was part of the run-up to the making of 2004's *The Alamo*).

There are many fine moments in the film, but all the competing plot lines and intermixing of time present and time past lead to some pretty slow passages. ★

Scene from
Lone Star (1996)
Courtesy Sony Pictures
Classics/Photofest
© Sony Pictures Classics.

The Alamo, 2004

Scene from *The Alamo* (2004) Courtesy Buena Vista Pictures.
Distribution/Photofest Courtesy Buena Vista Pictures.

The blowback from 9/11, Hollywood thought that another big Alamo epic was what the country needed. And so they set out to make the *ne plus ultra* of all Alamo movies, one that would be as historically accurate as possible. Ron Howard started out as director, but left for various reasons, and his replacement, Texas-born John Lee Hancock, stepped in. Hancock relied closely upon the advice of Texas history professors and other experts and together, they wrought another leaden ode to Texas' most famous battle.

Like most Alamo movies, this one focused on the triad, but with a difference. This time the emphasis was on the flawed nature of their characters. Travis had fled debts and a wife and child; Bowie had a distinctly unsavory background as slave trader and frontier brawler; and Crockett was looking for a fresh start after a disappointing Congressional career.

In director Hancock's hands, the Alamo offered a second chance. It offered them a shot at redemption, but they had to die to achieve it.

One problem, however, was the performances of some of the leading figures. Of Jason Patric's Bowie and Dennis Quaid's Sam Houston, a *New York Times* reviewer astutely observed, "Patric and especially Quaid . . . affect the kind of grim determination often found in laxative commercials." Only Billy Bob Thornton as Crockett shows a spark of energy.

Director Hancock, his screenwriters, his historian advisors, his set designer, and everybody connected with the film constantly harped on its accuracy. The set, near Dripping Springs, Texas, was praised as the most meticulously accurate one ever to be built. According to press releases, even the buttons on the Mexican uniforms were exact copies of the originals. The zeal for historical accuracy went so far as to distinguish between upper class Spanish spoken by officers and a more vernacular Spanish spoken by the soldiers. Yet who but a linguist with good hearing would ever take note of that fact? Then there was the obsession with depicting a long scene set in East Texas and conducted in Cherokee when Sam Houston has a conversation with Chief Bowles, his Indian friend. When this had to be cut from the final edit of the film, Hancock was sad and the historians were sad. Yet from a cinematic viewpoint, it is hard to imagine what possible value such a scene could have. In fact, all the scenes involving Sam Houston could have been cut.

But for all the film's vaunted commitment to historical accuracy, they were never going to get it right. Consider, for example, the memorable (and made-up) scene of Crockett playing a fiddle atop a wall of the Alamo. The tune is the "Mockingbird Quick Step," a version of "Listen to the Mockingbird." The problem, however, is that the song was not composed until 1855 (and is thus as anachronistic as "The Yellow Rose of Texas" in the 1937 *Heroes of the Alamo*)—exhibiting once again the danger of using historical veracity as the main yardstick of merit. And then there is this disturbing side-note: the Three Stooges used this tune as a theme song.

In the end, this *Alamo* is more of an expensive reenactment than a movie. ★

Schmaltz Across Texas

From the 1980s on, with the exception of flawed ambitious films like *Lone Star* and *The Alamo*, there has been a spate of minor films, emphasis on minor. Typical small films of the '80s include *Raggedy Man* (1981), scripted by Texan Bill Witliff; *Fandango* (1985), interesting for its homage to *Giant;* and *Nadine* (1987), written and directed by Texan Robert Benton.

From the nineties to now, Texas films have seemed to shrink even further. In two films written and directed by Richard Linklater, Texas all but disappears. *Slacker* (1991) is a glacially paced homage to Austin's counter-culture navel-gazing and its self-proclaimed embrace of weirdness. Linklater's second Austin-based film, *Dazed and Confused*

(1993) could have been filmed anywhere. The Plot Keyword feature of IMDB tells everything one needs to know about this tale of Seventies high school students: Pot Smoking/ Idealism/Muscle Car/Beer Drinking/Cult Favorite.

The small town ambience dominates many of the small films. One film that enjoyed far more attention than it deserved was *Dancer, Texas, Population 81* (1998). It told the story of four boys and a girl who are the only graduates of a tiny high school in far West Texas. Their goal in life—of the boys, anyway—is to visit L.A. when they finish high school, and to achieve this goal, they buy bus tickets at the age of nine and make a "sacred vow" (repeated endlessly, it seems) to travel together to Los Angeles. That is the premise of the film. All the adults are cretinous, and the high school kids are as sexless as newts.

Another weak film set in Down Home, Texas, is *Hope Floats* (1998). This sudser stars Sandra Bullock, who, following a divorce, returns from the bright lights, big city of Chicago to her home town of Smithville, Texas. Saddled with a whiny kid, an eccentric (but wise, of course) mother (Gena Rowlands, with a sappy southern accent), and a new boyfriend played ineptly by Harry Connick, Jr., Bullock pluckily comes to believe that hope floats, but so do cow patties.

Happy, Texas (1999) continued the trend of small-town Texas movies populated largely by eccentrics and supposedly loveable losers. The twist in this one is that two small-time criminals pose as a gay couple who specialize in training beauty contestants. Although they're not really gay, the manly sheriff, yuk yuk, comes out of the closet. *The Good Girl* (2002), which is solemn and "serious," takes place mostly inside a Wal-Mart type store and is worth seeing only if you want to watch Jennifer Aniston pretend to be poor. *Secondhand Lions* (2003) has a good cast, Robert Duvall and Michael Caine, but it too pegs its story on the premise of improbable eccentricities and sentimental comedy. Like the other small town Texas films, it reeks of inauthenticity.

One welcome exception, and something of a surprise hit, at least locally in Texas, was the documentary *Hands on a Hard Body* (1997). This film captured the lives, hopes, dreams, and voices of actual people who take part in a contest held in Longview, in East Texas. The contestants try to win a truck by outlasting their competitors. The rules are that each must touch the truck continuously until everybody but one, the winner, is left. There is more truth about people's real lives in this film than in most that deal with small-town Texas.

The best recent Texas film is one that goes to the heart of the Texas film tradition. Tommy Lee Jones' *The Three Burials of Melquiades Estrada* (2005), scripted by Guillermo Arriaga, fashions a compelling narrative out of elements of the Western, the border film, and ethnicity in the Southwest. Jones plays a hard-bitten ranch hand named Pete Perkins, who befriends an illegal vaquero, Melquiades Estrada. When Estrada is accidentally killed by a border patrol agent, Perkins sets out on a one-man journey to return his friend's body to Mexico, to the village and family that Estrada has spoken of but which in fact may not even exist. All the

The *Three Burials of Melquiades Estrada* (2005) Courtesy
EuropeCorp. Distribution/Photofest © EuropeCorp.

secondary roles are great, including January Jones as the
puzzled wife of Barry Pepper's border agent, Dwight
Yoakum as a dissolute Texas sheriff, and Levon Helm as an
old man ready to die but unable to find someone to assist
him. The film has a stark originality, great visual honesty in
its depiction of the material culture of the Southwest, and
a sure sense of character and redemption. Its only weakness
is that the more Estrada's body deteriorates, the more it
resembles Little Richard.

A much-anticipated Texas film with excellent blood
lines is 2007's *No Country for Old Men*, in which the Coen
brothers return to Texas to lense Cormac McCarthy's 2005
novel of the same name. Early promotional trailers promise
a revival of the wild beauty of the border country of far west
Texas and a character-driven narrative grounded in the old-
fashioned premise that evil exists and has its own inherent
and bloody logic. The film stars Tommy Lee Jones as Sheriff
Ed Tom Bell, Josh Brolin as Vietnam vet Llewelyn Moss,

No Country for Old Men
(2007) Courtesy Miramax
Films/Photofest
© Miramax Films.

and Javier Bardem as the unforgettable psychotic killer Anton Chigurh. All are receiving rave notices, as is the film in many early reviews.

One of the most interesting commentaries comes from Larry McMurtry. In "A River Runs Through It" (*Newsweek*, November 5, 2007), McMurtry cites Cormac McCarthy as "the literary master of the border." He describes the world of *No Country* with the authority of one who knows that world well: "It's not only no country for old men; it's no country for young or midde-aged men, either. It's also hard on dogs, and hardest on women."

McMurtry praises the film for its fidelity to the novel, approvingly quoting key lines from McCarthy's book that are used in the film. The sheriff is describing the collapse of ethics in his county: "It starts when you begin to overlook bad manners. Anytime you quit hearing 'Sir' and 'Ma'am,', the end is pretty much in sight." This film is a cinch to be better than Billy Bob Thornton's lame version of McCarthy's *All the Pretty Horses* (2000).

Next up, in what could be another profound film version of a McCarthy work is Ridley Scott's *Blood Meridian*, which is currently "in production" and pegged for release in 2009. Another Texas-themed film scheduled for release in 2007 seems to hark back to national stereotypes of Texans. *Charlie Wilson's War*, directed by Mike Nichols, is based on George Crile's book about Wilson, a colorful Texas Congressman who cooked up a military scheme to oust the Russians from Afghanistan back in the 1980s. Trailers of the film suggest broad stereotyping. Tom Hanks plays Wilson, and Julia Roberts plays Joanne Herring, a Texas socialite who helped finance the "war." *US Magazine* nailed the actress in its December 2007 review: "Roberts lards on her southern accent in a parade of ridiculous wigs, looking more like a tranny than a pretty woman." You can't judge a film by previews, but in the chat room of IMDB, viewers started raising questions about Roberts' accent and whether the film is a comedy or not.

Films like *The Three Burials* and *No Country For Old Men*, which draw upon traditional Texas themes and images, are likely to remain few and far between. In a century of Texas in the movies, the state has changed drastically, and many of its regional characteristics seem to have largely disappeared. University students from cities and suburbs often do not know the difference between a farm and a ranch, and many of them think that chopping cotton means to chop the cotton (not the weeds). With 82 percent of its booming population (23.5 million in 2006) residing in cities and suburbs, and with its steady influx of citizens from other parts of the U.S., the Texas that is seen in films like *Red River*, *Giant*, and *The Last Picture Show* seems to belong to another age. Which is OK, except that the recent films have a whole lot of trouble making modern Texas seem interesting and vital instead of corny and stupid.

The shooting started in 1900, and it hasn't stopped yet. As we move further into the twenty-first century, the appeal of Texas's past is receding, except when somebody talented comes forward and lights it up, deep in the heart of Hollywood. ★

About the Author

DON GRAHAM is the J. Frank Dobie Regents Professor of American English Literature at the University of Texas at Austin. He is the author of numerous books and articles, including *Cowboys and Cadillacs: How Hollywood Looks at Texas* (1983); *No Name on the Bullet: A Biography of Audie Murphy* (1989); *Giant Country: Essays on Texas* (1998); and *Kings of Texas: The 150-Year Saga of an American Ranching Empire* (2003). In 2003 Graham edited *Lone Star Literature: From the Red River to the Rio Grande*, and in 2007, *Literary Austin* (TCU Press). Graham has lived in Austin since the late 1970s. ★

State Fare: An Irreverent Guide
to Texas Movies
ISBN 978-0-87565-367-9
Case. $8.95
A Texas Small Book

ISBN 978-0-87565-367-9

50895

9 780875 653679